THE CRIT...

An Introduction to Looking at the Movies

Margo A. Kasdan, Ph.D.
Christine Saxton, Ph.D.

San Francisco State University

KENDALL/HUNT PUBLISHING COMPANY
Dubuque, Iowa

Copyright © 1988 by Kendall/Hunt Publishing Company

ISBN 0-8403-4920-3

All rights reserved. No part of this publication may be reproduced, stored in a retrieval system, or transmitted, in any form or by any means, electronic, mechanical, photocopying, recording, or otherwise, without the prior written permission of the copyright owner.

Printed in the United States of America
10 9 8 7 6 5 4 4 3 2 1

Contents

Preface **vii**

CHAPTER 1   The Visual Media   1

Introduction
Communication and Information
The Media
Visual Literacy
Realism: The Narrative Film
Persuasion Through Advertising
Persuasion and the Visual Media
Meaning and Response
Levels of Meaning

CHAPTER 2   The Camera Eye   13

A Historical Note
The Shot and the Frame
Distance
Angle
Camera Movement
The Lens/Focal Length/Focus
Laboratory Optical Processes
Special Effects

CHAPTER 3   Scene and Subject   37

Scene
    Mise En Scene
    The Set
    Blocking/Choreography
    Location
    Color
    Lighting
        A Historical Note
        The Technique of Lighting
Subject

      Actors and Acting
      Screen Acting
   Conclusion

CHAPTER 4 Editing 59

A Historical Note
Making the Film
The Shooting Ratio
Cutting : A Description
Classical Editing
The Match Cut
The Establishing Shot
Cross-Cutting
Transitions
The Jump-Cut
The Flashback and the Flash Forward
Soviet Montage
Montage in Hollywood
Point of View
The Point of View Shot
The Kuleshov Experiment in Editing
Point of View and the Narrator

CHAPTER 5 Sound 83

A Historical Note
Kinds of Sound
Synchronous and Non-Synchronous Sound
Music
Dialogue
Narration
Sound Effects

CHAPTER 6 Composition and Structure 105

Classical Composition
Perspective
Composition : Space
   Graphic Elements of Composition
   Composition in Film : The Frame
   Composition in Depth

    Composition and *Mise en Scene*
    Composition and Screen Size
    Dynamic Composition
Structure : Time
    Fiction and Non-fiction Film
    Structure : Narrative Film
    Structure : Documentary Film
    Structure : Experimental Film

CHAPTER 7   Making Meaning   135

Film as Language
Underlying Meaning
Connotation
Theme
Symbol
Motif
Allusion
Film Analysis: Little Big Man
Sequence Analysis
    Literal Meaning
    Cultural Connotation
    Textual Connotation

CHAPTER 8   Production, Distribution, Exhibition   159

A Historical Note
Four Factors of Change
The Legacy of the Blacklist
Hollywood *vs.* Television
Current Practice
    Production
    Distribution
    Exhibition
The Future

Afterword: A Critical Eye   175

Suggested Readings   177

Glossary   179

Index   185

Preface

These days, most people get information through the visual media. Almost everyone has had some exposure to TV and the movies; in the United States and, increasingly, all over the world they are a fact of life. Because they convey the values, assumptions, and ideas of our society, it is important to understand how they work. This book introduces the viewer—who is usually quite experienced at viewing, having watched hours, months, even years of TV and movies—to the vocabulary of film study and methods of interpretation. Knowing these things will help viewers become "film literate" and help them develop a "critical eye."

To reach these goals, this text sets out clearly and concisely the basic vocabulary of film. It also presents descriptive examples accompanied by pictures, and analyses of films so the beginning student can learn to recognize the way images convey information and stories, to think critically about what they see, and to interpret the images. In short, the text should enable students to see how movies produce meaning.

We would like to acknowledge the generous assistance of several colleagues and friends. For their critical reading and invaluable suggestions, Jan Gregory and Katherine Kovacs. For his perceptive culling of stills, Lester Glassner. For her solid research work, especially on current industry practices, Kim Collier. For helpful conversation, Russell Merritt. For her meticulous work on the frame enlargements, Dawn Hawk. For the generous contribution of their personal work, Nicole Hollander, Karen Holmes, Pat Ferrero, Trinh T. Minh-ha, Chris Beaver and Judy Irving. And especially, for his unflagging and enthusiastic support, intelligent advice, and technical assistance with the computers, Gary Kluge.

CHAPTER 1
The Visual Media

If you had gone to France just thirty years ago, you would have found that, unlike the United States, it had only two TV channels, they broadcast only about 6 hours per day, and the government-controlled media agency chose all the programming. Many things would have struck you in those days as the opposite from things in this country. For example, French TV had no ads, but before every show at the movies they showed short film ads for everything from socks and shirts to ice cream and candy.

Even if you had gone in 1970, you would have found the situation more or less unchanged. By that time, one or two more TV channels had been added along with a few more hours in the broadcast day. You would have seen some movies, French ones, but mostly the same type of programs, most of them cultural, shown without interruption with only a few minutes of advertising grouped at the end of the programs. And if you were feeling a little homesick, you could always go to see an American movie (with French subtitles, of course) playing in a special "art" movie house.

In 1987, ORTF, the French government media agency that controls radio and television broadcasting, sold two channels to private commercial companies which began to broadcast American programs: rock videos, sitcoms, especially the very popular series, "Dallas" and "Dynasty," game shows, quiz shows, and a complete range of films, including American ones. All the programs and films were dubbed into French.

To enable the channels to pay their way, the private companies introduced at least 12 minutes per hour of advertising interruptions. Amazingly, rather than scaring away people who had never before had to suffer through breaks in their programs, the "new" TV was very popular. Now, suddenly, the French were talking as fluently of J.R. (pronounced "Gee Air"), the "Streets of San Francisco" (pronounced "Saun Franseesco"), "market share," "exposure," and "advertising revenue," as they did about the Eiffel Tower and champagne. And you would have found, if you had visited, that cowboy boots and hats were as fashionable as the blue jeans (pronounced "lay bloo-djeen") that have long been popular with Europeans.

The situation in Italy mirrors the one in France. And in many other countries American TV shows and movies are wide-spread, their position powerful: in Germany "Dallas" and "Dynasty" are dubbed into German. In Libya, where many women still wear their faces covered and divorce is not permitted, "Dallas," with its marital intrigues, is dubbed into Arabic. In Japan, where the family is strongly respected, "Dynasty" with its vicious family conflicts, is dubbed into Japanese. Because of the impact of these and other American programs, values and attitudes are being influenced all over the world. For example, in the area of food, in Europe, where people never before ate a great deal of beef, hamburger and barbeque restaurants have become popular, largely as part of the "Texas" theme that has gained attention through the TV shows.

Communication and Information

But at another very important level, thanks to technological developments in telecommunications, information travels faster and farther than ever before. The Chernobyl nuclear accident, Palestinian demonstrations on the West Bank, the Challenger disaster, revelations of the National Security Council's covert activities in Iran and Central America became common international knowledge almost instantly, and in some cases were actually seen "live" via satellite.

Information about people, in particular movie and TV stars and their lifestyles, is readily available through the media. Magazines supply an audience with information to feed its curiosity about media figures. It is pretty safe to say that many people are more familiar with Michael Jackson's plastic surgery and Madonna's marital activities than with the location of Washington D.C. on a map. Of course, movie stars have long been the subject of gossip and attention and in the United States, *People* and *US* magazines (or for more extravagant tastes, the *National Enquirer* and *Star*) regularly publish stories about their lives. But the unprecedented number of people around the world who know about the stars, who saw the Live-Aid concert or who regularly watch MTV and know the latest songs, demonstrates the vastness of the new horizons opened up by international telecommunications.

The fact that other countries see so much of our media products means that the impact of American culture is very great. Then, too, the obvious effects of American media, like the blossoming of McDonald's hamburger restaurants around the world, are *signs* of less obvious influences like the steady conversion of European television from a cultural entity to a merchandising one.

When we travel in other countries we can see quite clearly the effects of the media on people's daily lives. That impact is not so noticeable in our own culture because we take it for granted as "natural" and do not question it. Yet the media influence everyone, everywhere. All our lives we have watched TV and movies, mainly for entertainment and information; they are a source of pleasure, escape, even companionship—a constant part of people's lives. We must realize, though, that the media also have the power to influence and control.

The Media

Observers say that the public in today's world "consumes" the media as never before. But is it only "today"? For years, people have been buying newspapers and magazines by the millions and listening to thousands of hours of radio. The difference is that nowadays, most of all they "use" the *visual* media. And, not surprisingly, Americans, as they do with other kinds of resources, use more than anyone else. The average American family watches more than seven hours of television a day, 99% of American homes have at least one TV set, 39% have two, and more than 80 million people are likely to be watching television on any given evening. This is a medium that has become a large part of many people's daily life and has a great effect on the way those lives are led.

Even though people all over the world are watching a great deal of television they also continue to enthusiastically attend movies. In Europe, people line up for the latest movie releases and movie theaters are flourishing. In the United States, in 1987 about 123 million people went to the movies, more than ever before. In addition, the videotape sales and rental business is flourishing; a growing proportion of those millions watching television every night are watching videotape releases of movies.

Some fans return to (or rent) their favorite movies over and over, never tiring of characters, stories, music, and particular scenes. Some come to know the dialogue and images so well they can provide a scene by scene description while they listen to a recording of the soundtrack. Sometimes the audience participates actively. At viewings of CASABLANCA (1942) or HAROLD AND MAUDE (1972), viewers regularly call out the well-known and well-loved lines of dialogue, and at the ROCKY HORROR PICTURE SHOW (1975) fans dress up like the actors and mimic or enact on the stage *in front* of the screen the action *on* the screen.

Observers note somewhat nervously that contemporary society has become a **visual culture**, *dependent upon looking at images rather than on reading words.* It is pretty safe to say that society will always be dependent to an extent upon writing, but perhaps less these days, constantly exposed as it is to images—on television, in movies, photographs, newspapers, advertisements, magazines, on billboards, product labels, record jackets, among many other locations.

Some critics blame the visual media, especially television, for America's decline in literacy because, they argue, people would rather watch moving images passively than read words, which requires activity

Figure 1. Rocky Horror Picture Show (d. Jim Sharman, 1975). Janet and Brad, house hunting, find themselves confronted with the weird inhabitants of the house of their dreams. This campy musical became a cult film that has continued in midnight screenings for over 15 years after initial release.

and work. One thing is certain: **the widespread power of the visual media around the world has made it necessary to study them, to understand them, and to see how they work**—in other words, to become **visually literate**.

Visual Literacy

Let us consider for a moment the idea of literacy. To be literate means more than just being able to read and pronounce the words on the page. To be *functionally* literate a reader must be able to grasp the meaning, first of each word, then of all the words combined, and to understand a sentence and a paragraph. To be *fully* literate involves even more: the reader must be able to detect the underlying structure of a piece of writing, to recognize how s/he is being persuaded, to understand the implications of what has been said. The ability to *detect structure*, to *recognize persuasion*, and to *understand meaning* is the basis of understanding all written communication.

Media experts occasionally object to applying the terms "reading" (as in "reading a film") and "literacy" (as in "visual literacy") to *pictures*, and in a way they are correct because, after all, the word *literate* comes from *letters* and has to do with words and language. Then, too, people grasp visual information differently than written information. But since there is no equivalent word for pictures, no "picturate," and "visually literate" is handy and understandable, it makes sense to let *literacy* mean for visual media what it does for writing: **the ability to understand sequences of moving images combined with sound and to follow a story or understand information as told through those sequences**. The process of making meaning in visual media requires two operations just as writing does: first, the filmmaker arranges the images into combinations that make sense. Then the visually literate viewers extract meaning from the images.

Most people have been watching movies and television since they were very young, so at an early age they learned to make sense of a visual story line. Partly as a result of that familiarity, they assume that understanding images is not at all like understanding a book. "It's automatic," they say, "basically just like looking at real life, not like reading where you have to think about the words. A camera just reproduces what you put in front of it." And they are at least partly right. We do absorb images in a more direct way than we do words. And we do understand much of what we see on the screen because it is familiar to us from our experience of the world. But the opposite is also true: we know aspects of the world only because we have seen them before on a screen. Where, besides in the movies and on television, have you seen spaceships, phasars, droids, wookies, or high-tech control panels for communication with alien life forms? When, for that matter, was the last time you visited the Middle East, or the mountains of Nepal? What about NASA's laboratories? When was the last time you saw a bank robbery and all those marvellous gadgets they use that open safes? Or a car chase, a stagecoach or even a cowboy?

Realism: The Narrative Film

But let us ask a few more questions. What happens when we look at a feature film that tells a *story*? Does the film show only what was in front of the camera? Do events happen in the film exactly as in real life? Let us look at the beginning of a simple movie, STAND BY ME (1986). This movie is basically pretty "realistic": the kids are recognizably regular kids; the town looks like most any small town; the story is plausible (see fig. 2). But let's take a closer look.

The movie opens with a wide view of fields and trees, a Toyota Land Cruiser parked on the side of the road, quite far away. Suddenly "we" are closer to the car and then inside it, in the passenger seat, looking at the main character, Gordon (Richard Dreyfuss). In an instant "we" have somehow travelled at least a hundred yards, managed to reach the opposite side of the car and get inside. Equally remarkable, Gordon's lips aren't moving, yet we *hear* him speaking as he gazes out the front window of the car. What are we hearing? His thoughts, of course, through that time-honored convention of the movies known as the *"voice-over"*. While we hear him reminiscing about his past we are treated to yet another trick—we *see* his memories when, through an impossible leap in space and time, we are transported back about twenty-seven years to 1959 and to a little town in Oregon, through another time-honored movie convention, the *flashback*.

So far, the organization of the segment is fairly standard and we understand it perfectly well since most of us have seen hundreds of flashback sequences and heard countless voice-overs. In fact, *we are already "reading" the film*. Let's accept this first part of the film even though it does not adhere strictly to reality and go on to the next part that takes place in Castle Rock, Oregon, in 1959. Here, too, at first the action seems to be very recognizable and even more continuous, more like "real life."

Figure 2. Stand by Me (d. Rob Reiner, 1985). Every element works to make the shot look "realistic." "Regular" kids, simple clothes, no make-up. The angle is almost straight on and the medium distance reproduces what the eye normally sees. Linear perspective is marked by the diagonal of the railroad tracks leading back into the frame suggesting the distance the boys have travelled. The line of the tracks contrasts with the gazes and the outstretched arm.

Young Gordie, in a drugstore, picks up a magazine and pays for it. But, then, in not so much as an instant, we find ourselves outside on the street and Gordie is strolling out the door coming toward "us." How did he get from the cash register to the sidewalk so fast? And, for that matter, how did "we" get all the way down the street so that "we" could look back at him? Clearly, even this most standard opening is *not* like real life.

It is pretty clear once we think about what we are seeing that movie action and events really are not at all like our own life experience. They only *seem* to be because we have grown accustomed to *seeing* them through the camera eye and *reading* meaning into them within a story. But most of us actually understand only a little about what we see and don't really detect structure or recognize that every image sets out to *persuade*. And if we never question what we see, we are susceptible to the power of the media.

Persuasion Through Advertising

Advertisers know better than almost anyone just how powerful the image can be. For one thing, ad agencies spend millions on market research into audience preferences and responses to visual images, and more millions on ad campaigns that when successful, generate billions in return. It is no secret that ads are designed to influence their audience. It is a better kept secret that *the movies and TV are also designed to influence their viewers*. Audiences are increasingly seen as "target" groups (like consumers of food and drinks), their responses registered and quantified. If it emerges statistically that a market exists among "kids-14-to-17-living-in-urban-areas-with-a-disposable-income-of-$6000-a-year," then films and TV programs geared specifically to that "target group" will very likely be produced. The purpose of an ad is to sell a specific product; the purpose of a film is to sell itself; the purpose of a television program is to sell both. TV is, of course, a vehicle for broadcasting paid advertisements in order to generate shareholder profits, but television shows also sell indirectly. Although the content of any single show has little to do with a specific product, it *models behavior* and so, inevitably, sets up the desire for many products, like cars, cigarettes, and fashionable clothes through its presentation of exciting settings and attractive, stylish people.

Movies, on the other hand, since they do not take commercial breaks are less involved than TV shows with direct sales. Nevertheless, in their own way movies sell a style of life and are as dependent on affecting an audience as any advertisement. Most obviously, the box office receipts must show profit so people have to be drawn in to see the movies. Ads produce meaning in a controlled way, using words and images geared to the one purpose of selling a sponsor's product. As we shall see, movies (and TV programs) also use words and images in a controlled way but geared to the purpose of involving the viewers to keep them coming back to see more.

Persuasion and the Visual Media

The visual media resemble advertisements in that they all use accepted ideas about the desirable characteristics associated with groups: femininity and masculinity, youth and old-age, beauty, success, and many other attributes. Accepted ideas portrayed in characters allow the viewer to quickly recognize "types" in advertisements but also in TV shows and movies. The point is illustrated by any cigarette ad. Marlboro, for example, models rugged masculinity, represented by the cowboy. Virginia Slims presents the young, active, independent woman and Benson & Hedges offers itself as the cigarette of a sophisticated and affluent group. One doesn't need to actually belong to any of these groups; one only needs to *want* to. There's a good chance that if a smoker is attracted by the image in the ad and does identify with the characters, the next time s/he buys cigarettes, Marlboro, Virginia Slims or Benson & Hedges will come to mind but without the buyer's recalling exactly why. This is just what the company that produces all three brands, R. J. Reynolds, wants since it has spent millions creating a more or less unconscious mental association between the brands of cigarettes and particular character traits and lifestyles.

To read an ad at another level does require work but finally *gives the reader/viewer power of judgement over the image.* We have already noted that ads have a more direct purpose than either films or television shows, but, as we shall see, similar treatment of characters and setting is involved in all of these forms. Persuasion is one strategy, the success of which, in films and TV, usually depends on esthetic standards as well as entertainment appeal. But no image ever appears on either the large or the little screen that does not appeal in some way to the viewer's desires, reason, or respect for authority. What's more, visual images, like advertising, depend on a response to the myths, values, and traditional assumptions of the culture and society.

Meaning and Response

Two basic questions for understanding media are: *how do they make meaning* and *how does that meaning affect the viewer.* Now, advertisers, television producers, and filmmakers all try to provoke a response in the viewer. In the case of film and TV, the intention may not always be to persuade the viewer to buy or act. But every sequence of images tries to make the viewer understand, respond, or at the very least, go on watching.

To be **functionally literate visually** is to *know* that there is an element of persuasion in the material. To be **fully literate visually** is to *detect* the underlying structure of a visual work, whether it is a TV commercial, a news show, a sit com, or a movie; it is to *recognize* the means of persuasion; it is to *perceive the strategies* being used; it is to *understand the underlying persuasive elements*. It is, finally, to have developed "a critical eye."

The opening scenes of STAND BY ME show that even realistic image sequences are not really "real." They are *constructed* out of shots and are meant to generate response in very specific ways. The essential point is that *all media are made up of bits of information that are bound together to produce a meaningful whole. All images are significant* and in order to understand the significance, viewers must scan for and process various kinds of information. If the viewer does not understand one picture, he or she will not be able to put that one picture together with others in a way that makes sense. Images must be "read" and even a single picture, the simplest, most straightforward one, requires a reading.

Levels of Meaning

Form and content operate in all mediums, and auditory message operates in several but since they combine in a complex way in film and on TV let us explain them here briefly.

1. Form: In the movies and on TV shows, the *form* is always the photographic image. TV can be divided by format: situation comedy, mini-series, talk show, news show, etc. Films are divided first into two broad areas: non-fiction—documentaries—and fiction. Fiction films or, as we call them, *feature* films are divided into various *genres*—Westerns, Horror films, Musicals, Comedies and Science Fiction, among others. Animation and the experimental cinema may be either fiction or non-fiction but they are visually distinctive.

Fiction depends on a whole tradition of story-telling which in cinema led to the development of certain specific conventions. Non-fiction films, on the other hand, rarely used the many visual conventions of fiction filmmaking but recently documentaries and news programs are beginning to use dramatic structures, and even the experimental cinema, the "freest" form, often has certain "narrative" aspects. (More on this in Chapter 6.)

2. Content: Films, like ads, depend upon traditional assumptions, expectations and values. Viewers know how to read meaning based on participation in their culture and specific experience with the media. Deeper levels of meaning also come into play as a direct result of the way the film has been organized. We will examine levels of meaning and structure as we study the different aspects of film production and viewing. (More on this in Chapter 6 and 7.)

3. Auditory Message: Both film and TV use dialogue, narration, sound effects, and music to guide audience response to the action, to provide information about future action, and to shape the way in which the audience will receive subsequent images and sound effects. A common example of the guiding and shaping power of narration is the voice of the TV news commentator who explains the news that is seen on the screen. (More on this in Chapter 5.)

We have only introduced the visual media here and touched upon the way they make meaning. The following chapters will discuss in detail the methods that make film "work." We will concentrate on the film medium throughout the rest of this book, first because it is recognized as an important art form and, secondly, because video and television techniques and structures, evolved out of film processes and so it is the basis of *all* "visual language."

One question remains: Why go to all the trouble to figure out "underlying meanings" when you can "just sit back and enjoy the show?" We would propose that this kind of exploration can make films more interesting and therefore, more fun. Many more ideas and much more information can be found in almost any movie than a superficial viewing allows. As with all the arts, the more we discover about the aesthetic principles governing the work, the richer our experience of that work will be. And finally, as we have emphasized in this chapter, an examination of the images leads to an understanding of how the images use values, social expectations, and widely-shared emotional and psychological needs to affect viewers. If using the media is a source of power for politicians, advertisers, and also film and TV producers, then **fully understanding the way those media work gives power back to the viewer.**

CHAPTER 2
The Camera Eye

The **camera** makes movies possible. Most of us, having grown up with a still camera and photo albums full of snapshots, maybe even a Super-8 or video camera, are familiar with what a camera does: it takes pictures. In technical terms, *it mechanically records an image onto a plastic strip coated with a light-sensitive material called* **emulsion.** A still camera takes only one image at a time and records several different images on different areas of the strip of film. The movies are not really as different from snapshots as they look. In fact, the movie camera does not really reproduce movement at all. Motion pictures are made up of hundreds of still images which, when shown in rapid succession (18 frames per second for Super-8 millimeter, 24 frames per second for 16, 35, and 70 mm film) produce the *illusion* of movement. The illusion is based on a visual phenomenon called **persistence of vision:** *the image stays on the retina of the eye for a split second after the image has disappeared from sight.* "Persistence of vision" is actually the basis of "movies."

The film viewer can see only what the director chooses to show through the camera lens. That statement may seem self-evident but when we see a movie in this "age of mechanical reproduction," we often imagine that "objective reality" is being filmed without human intervention. It is

Figure 3. Saving the Proof (Karen Holmes, 1985). The phenomenon of perception known as persistence of vision keeps the image on the retina for a fraction of a second so when the film is run at appropriate speed for its size, the images look continuous. (18 frames/second and 24 frames/second).

easy to forget that the director's choices, made from behind the camera, determine what appears on the screen before our eyes. *The fact is that we "go" where the camera goes and we "see" what and how it allows us to see.*

Where we go and what we see are determined by the **"set-up"** of a shot. The set-up involves several steps. Usually the director and cinematographer start by deciding *where to place the camera*—how close, how far, how high, how low; and then they decide how to shoot—*when to move the camera, when not to, what kind of movement to use* (see fig. 4). The possibilities are almost infinite and the decisions made turn out to be very significant.

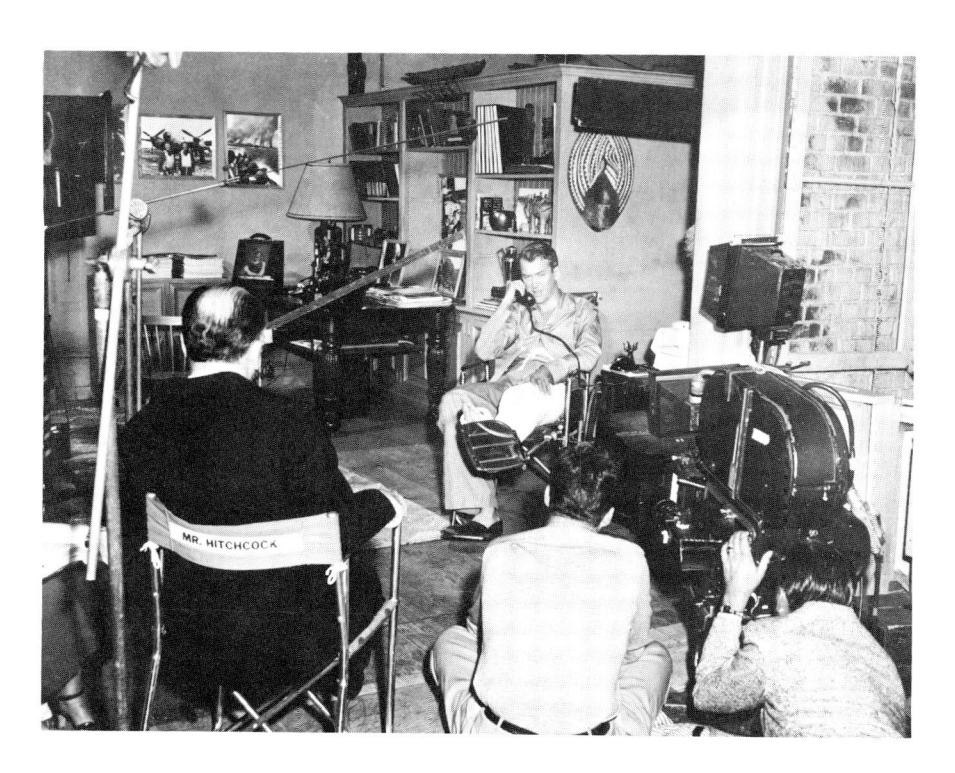

Figure 4. The set-up. Lights, camera angle, and distance are selected. The microphone is placed. Here the actor is included so the set-up extends to the entire "mise en scene," the arrangement of *all* elements in front of the camera (see Chapter 6).

14

A Historical Note

In the early days of cinema, dramatic action was shot from a fixed distance from the subject. It was not easy to move the camera and when a director did move it, he did so to get a better view of the action and the background. But very quickly, pioneering directors, like Thomas Ince and D.W. Griffith, realized that the **angle** on and the **distance** from the subject determined how the scene and the actors looked. That in turn affected both the viewers' understanding of the story and their response to it. Directors soon began to plan camera placement with great care. To achieve meaningful results, they filmed from every imaginable angle and distance. They juxtaposed differing shots which gave the viewer the illusion of moving, free and invisible, among the characters, on the set, at the very center of the action. Most important, they *varied* angle and distance, an enormous leap in film methodology which continues to be important in cinematography to the present day.

The Shot and the Frame

The two basic elements of cinematography are the **shot** and the **frame**. The cameraperson *composes the image* within the limits these factors imply, with the goal of bringing out details of action, character, and mood.

The **shot** is the *primary unit of filmmaking. It is a single, uncut length of film that records an action without interruption*, just like a strip of many snapshots taken with a still camera.

The **frame** refers both to the *edges of the image* which act like a picture frame, and to *one single image on the film stock*, out of possibly hundreds that make up one single shot. The cinematographer *frames* the shot, first by *choosing subject matter and then by choosing distance, angle, and lighting.*

Distance

The first decision that must be made, once the subject matter is determined, is what **distance** to shoot from. Depending on what information or emotion is to be conveyed, the director and cinematographer will choose a **close-up**, a **medium shot**, or a **long shot**. The distances of these shots are always *relative* to one another and *measured according to human* *scale, that is, by how much of the figure is registered within the frame.* Filmmakers typically define the degrees of distance as follows:

Close-up. *The camera records an area in which a person's head (or an object) fills the screen so there is no background.* In fiction films the close-up is most often used to show a character's feelings, responses, and emotions, or else objects of special significance (a gun or a cup of poisoned coffee, for example). In documentaries it is used to "get close" to the people in interviews or to show details of objects or processes in the subject matter being filmed. In both cases, the close-up contributes to the meaning of an image through the feeling of intimacy and intensity it conveys to the viewer (see fig. 5).

Medium Shot. *The camera records an area equal to the height of a seated figure or a figure from the waist up* (see fig. 6). It is commonly used for scenes in which both dialogue and a limited context are important. (In 1911, a French director named Victorin Jasset noticed the frequent use of what they called a medium shot by American directors and named it the "American Shot." Actually it is slightly fuller than the accepted definition of medium shot because it includes the figure from

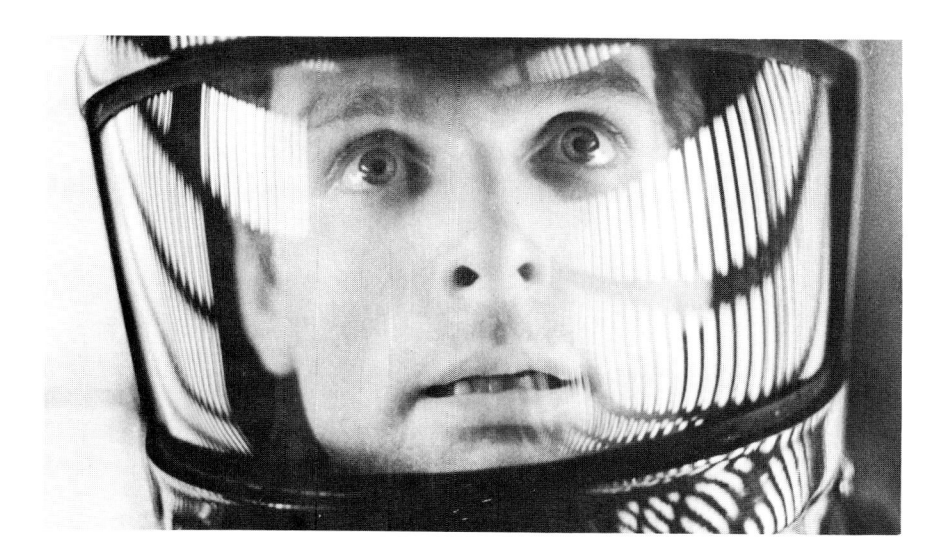

Figure 5. 2001: A Space Odyssey (d. Stanley Kubrick, 1968). The close-up. Camera distances are always relative. A close-up of a single figure may border on an extreme close-up as in this shot; the helmet and the patterns of shadow reflected in it limit the area of frame and emphasize the face giving the shot a rich texture. A close-up in wide angle like this one is relatively rare.

Figure 6. Dark Victory (d. Edmund Goulding, 1939). The medium shot. The height of a seated figure. This "two-shot" is realistic in style, perfectly unobtrusive: medium distance, eye level angle, normal lens, soft lighting, approximating the way the eye sees (except for the hairlights).

about mid-calf. In France the "medium" shot is still called the *"plan americain."*)

Filmed plays, like Howard Hawks's HIS GIRL FRIDAY (1940) and Richard Thorpe's NIGHT MUST FALL (1937), among many others, relied on this shot as did such melodramas as NOW VOYAGER (1942) and DARK VICTORY (1939). Most dialogue, whether conversation or exposition, has traditionally been shot at medium distance so that the viewer's attention is not diverted from the dialogue.

Long Shot. *The camera records an area the height of a standing figure, usually including extensive background, which emphasizes the relation between the figure and its surroundings.* The **full shot** is a more confined type of long shot, one in which *a figure fills the screen from the top to the bottom of the frame.* At this distance, the actors (or real people in documentaries) can make their physical stance and gestures noticeable while being close enough so their facial expressions are visible (see fig. 7).

* * *

Figure 7. The Gold Rush (d. Charlie Chaplin, 1925). The Little Tramp, prospecting for gold, wanders around in a snowy wilderness. The full-shot is important to many comedians because it allows them to use the whole body for comic expression.

These are the basic definitions of **distance**. The divisions depend on the cinematographer's preferences and style so the terminology is somewhat imprecise. Critics have tried to quantify the exact distances involved in all possible shots, but if we extend our list just a little to include the **medium close shot**, which is *between a close-up and a medium shot*, **extreme long shot**, which produces a *tiny figure in a great expanse of background*, and the **extreme close-up**, which shows *a detail of a face or object*, we will have covered the most commonly used terms.

Angle

Along with the choice of distance, the filmmaker must make a decision about the **angle**. *The angle is the position of the camera in relation to the subject and may be high or low, or at eye-level.*

The **straight-on, eye-level shot** *seems to show no visible angle*. The camera assumes the place of an average viewer standing up. The shot is so familiar that it seems "neutral," reproducing as it does, the scope that corresponds most closely to the way we normally see (see fig. 6).

The **low angle shot** *places the camera lower than the subject and by looking up at it, him, or her produces a towering figure or object.* The shot is used expressively to suggest dominance, power, or authority (see fig. 8) and, depending on the purposes of the director, may give a heroic, menacing, oppressive, or mythic effect.

An example of just what camera placement can mean occurred during the 1987 Iran-Contra hearings. An editorial on the hearings in the June 21, 1987 issue of *The New Yorker* magazine, pointed out that a camera placed just below the witness table produced an angle that completely reversed the situation the reporters, sitting in the hearing room, experienced. For them, the witness, Lieutenant-Colonel Oliver North, was seated down low and the committee up high in the usual position of a suspect before the judges. But the low placement of the camera meant that the television viewers saw North from a low angle, which made him look heroic. For a time, this witness, under investigation and eventually indicted, became something of a national hero, proving once again, in case we had any doubts, how powerful media presentation is.

Figure 8. Citizen Kane (d. Orson Welles, 1941). The low angle oblique shot. Kane is dwarfed by his own picture just as the man is by his image.

The response created by TV illustrates an important aspect of what we called "visual literacy" in Chapter 1. Viewers responded to Lieutenant-Colonel North according to a conventional image of a movie-star hero, perhaps, in this case, to a "John Wayne doing his patriotic duty." By placing a camera at a low angle, an *effect* favorable to North was created. No one is suggesting that the TV cameramen were predisposed to him and purposely put a camera in a spot that would show him in a good light. But even without intending to make a hero of him, they used an angle that was an important factor in doing just that.

Another scene that illustrates the heroic effect of the low angle is the attempted lynching in John Ford's YOUNG MR. LINCOLN (1939). In the film, Lincoln is standing on the jailhouse steps, holding back a lynch mob. The shots of Lincoln are taken from a low angle (suggesting the point of view of the mob looking up at Lincoln and also that of the movie viewer). The angle makes him look powerful and larger than life; when he successfully stops the lynch-mob, his mythic stature is underlined.

John Frankenheimer's 1962 film THE MANCHURIAN CANDIDATE contains several examples of they way intense angles produce tension and menace. Raymond Shaw (Lawrence Harvey) is seen in a strong low angle just before he carries out, under hypnosis, the command to kill his father-in-law. His oppressive, domineering mother, Mrs. Iselin (Angela Lansbury) is shown in several extreme low angle shots that suggest her power.

A contemporary example of the low angle to produce a feeling of menace appears in THE UNTOUCHABLES (1987). Al Capone (Robert DeNiro) framed in a low angle, moves slowly around a table at which his gang is seated. He pretends to be talking to them about baseball but he is really talking about loyalty and teamwork. He ends his comments by using the bat he is carrying to crush the skull of one of the henchmen he considers a traitor, finally carrying out the menace that has been threatened by the low camera angle.

The **high angle shot** *places the camera higher than the subject and looks down at it, him, or her suggesting the helplessness and vulnerability of the subject* (see fig. 9). In PSYCHO (1960), Alfred Hitchcock showed the murder of the unsuspecting detective, Arbogast (Martin Balsam), in a high angle shot. In the scene, the detective, searching for the woman who has run off with stolen money, mounts the stairs of the old house behind the Bates motel. The camera is at the top of the stairs, looking down at him, as he calmly begins to climb. An attacker suddenly swoops down on him, stabbing him and he falls backwards, down the stairs, bleeding and

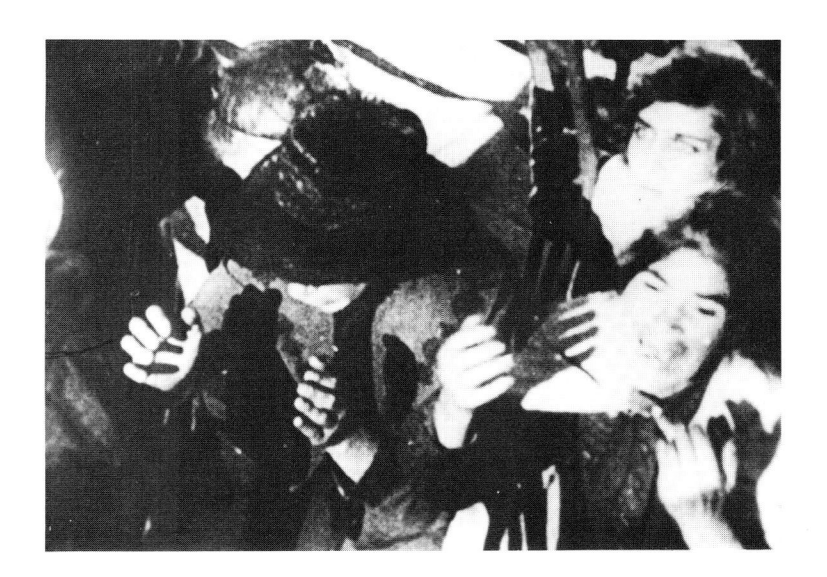

Figure 9. The Battleship Potemkin (d. Sergei Eisenstein, 1925). The Odessa Steps sequence. A group of women plead with Cossack soldiers. The high angle emphasizes their vulnerability and their demeaned position as they beg the soldiers to stop shooting the people of Odessa.

dying. Hitchcock's stated reason for using the high angle shot was to prevent the audience from seeing the murderer before he was ready to reveal "whodunit." In addition, the high angle also makes Arbogast look vulnerable to attack from above, heightening the menace and suspense set up by the brutal murder in the shower.

The **extreme high angle shot** or **bird's eye view** *places the camera directly overhead "like a bird," looking straight down at the scene."* It distorts the image slightly because the angle foreshortens the perspective; it is not often used since people rarely see from that angle. Again, PSYCHO offers an example. Norman Bates (Anthony Perkins) goes up to his mother's room to take her to the cellar. The camera moves upward paralleling Norman as he climbs the stairs and it continues up as he enters the room and then reappears. By using a bird's eye shot of Norman carrying his mother, Hitchcock prevents the audience from seeing what Norman is really carrying and, at the same time, subtly reinforces the bird motif that has already been set up in the narrative.

The **oblique angle** *is produced when the camera films while tilted so that when the film is projected, the subject is on a diagonal.* This type of shot is usually used to suggest tension or trouble. Towards the end of THE 39 STEPS (1935), Richard Hannay (Robert Donat), who has been following clues to discover a spy ring, realizes that the music hall performer, Mr. Memory, is the conduit of the secret information. At Mr. Memory's performance, Hannay calls out, "What are the thirty-nine steps?" An oblique angle on Mr. Memory visually conveys his tension, the struggle between his compulsion as a professional to answer the question and his certainty that the answer will cost him his life.

THE MANCHURIAN CANDIDATE provides another example of the oblique shot. Just after Raymond murders his father-in-law and his wife, the director cuts to Major Ben Marco (Frank Sinatra) coming home carrying a newspaper with the headline about the murder. The tilted framing on him as he enters the apartment, conveys his inner tension—relief at the proof of Raymond's "sickness" and horrified guilt for not having stopped him.

Camera angle cannot be separated from distance. A low angle shot from far away will be less obvious than one taken from a medium or close range; a close shot, on the other hand, will sharpen a high or low angle because *distance alters the intensity of the angle.* Orson Welles is renowned for his use of extreme low angle close-up shots that call attention to the place of the camera. In CITIZEN KANE (1941), for example, Kane's old friend, Jedediah Leland (Joseph Cotton), comes into the newspaper office, drunk, after Kane's election defeat. The camera is so low that Kane's legs seem to be elephant size and dominate the frame (see fig. 10).

Along with *conveying or withholding information*, **camera angle** almost always *carries a certain emotional effect* and often a judgement on the characters and actions involved. In THE MANCHURIAN CANDIDATE, faced by Mrs. Iselin in a low angle, we are repelled and frightened by her evil power over her son; in PSYCHO, looking at the defenseless Arbogast from a high angle shot, we are frightened for him.

In these two examples, meaning is presented from a **point of view** that does not "belong" to a single character; it is supposedly "objective," an outsider's point of view. More often, however, a shot does represent a character's point of view. That view is conveyed in the **point of view shot** or **subjective shot** or **first-person shot**, named precisely because *the camera takes the "subjective" view of a character* in the story. The shot may be taken from almost any distance or angle as long as it corresponds to the viewer's knowledge of the character's location. *It presents a character's personal point of view by showing the audience what the character is supposed to be looking at, and how s/he responds to the object viewed.*

Figure 10. Citizen Kane. Jedediah Leland arrives in the newspaper office drunk, after Kane's defeat at the polls. The extreme low angle in deep focus (as most of the film is) distorts the towering figure of Kane.

The **subjective shot** may be considered a specific type of point-of-view shot since *it often recreates (along with the visual perspective), the character's physical and/or emotional experience.* One example appears in F.W. Murnau's THE LAST LAUGH (1924). The protagonist, an aging hotel doorman, suffers a hangover and, as he struggles to get ready for work, we see, through his eyes, a world in which objects are out of focus, distorted, and weaving (see fig. 34). Another example, in NOTORIOUS (1946), shows Alicia (Ingrid Bergman), the morning after a drunken spree opening her eyes to see Dev (Cary Grant) approaching her—upside down. Near the end of the film, the subjective shot is repeated; this time the tone is no longer one of amusement as we see that Alicia's vision is, once again, distorted—but by the effects of poison.

Point of view, whether in the form of the point-of-view shot, the subjective shot, or the so-called "objective" shot (although *the camera always has a point of view*) is perhaps the most important strategy of storytelling in general and of film narrative in particular. We will discuss the issue in more detail in Chapter 4.

Camera Movement

Once the *position of the camera—distance, angle, and lighting—* have been determined, the **set-up** is nearly complete. (More about lighting in Chapter 3.) Now another decision must be made; should the shot remain **fixed** or would the action and meaning of the shot be better served by **camera movement**? And if so, what kind of camera movement?

The Pan shot or Panning shot. (The name comes from the word "panorama.") *The camera is mounted on a non-moving base and films while pivoting on its axis, along the line of the horizon from left to right or right to left*. The pan is the simplest of camera movements, like a person looking to the left or to the right, moving only her/his head. The shot may be used to follow action as it moves beyond the limits of the frame and to reveal new information.

In THE MANCHURIAN CANDIDATE a simple, continuous pan (eventually revealed to be part of a dream) begins with a shot of a group of American soldiers seated on a stage. The camera pans slowly around the room, over an audience made up of ladies listening to a garden club lecture. The camera continues panning through a full circle, passing the soldiers a second time, and ends on the audience which has now become a group of Russian and Chinese military officials listening to a lecture on brainwashing. The effect is dramatic.

Variations on the pan are: the **Swish pan** that *follows the same horizontal movement as the pan but so rapidly that the image blurs*. Not very common, it is usually used as a transitional device from one spot to another, or one time period to another. Another is the **tilt** *where a camera is mounted on a fixed base and moves either up or down* instead of panning laterally (from side to side).

The Travelling shot, Tracking shot, Trucking shot. *Travelling is the general term for any moving shot.* Recording a landscape from a moving train or car with a fixed camera that moves only because of the movement of the vehicle on which it is situated is the simplest means of achieving movement and was used as early as 1899 in Louis Lumiere's *The Grand Canal in Venice.*

In a **tracking shot** *the camera films while it moves parallel to the movement of the subject being filmed.* It was originally called a tracking shot because *tracks* were laid on the set along which the camera mounted on wheels moved. Conventionally, travelling shots follow, in smooth, fluid motion, significant characters and important actions of the story (see fig. 11).

These days the camera is mounted on a vehicle designed so it can move freely either on tracks or, more commonly, on rubber wheels. The miniaturized vehicle is called a **dolly** and the better ones provide a cushioned motion that preserves the fluidity traditionally considered essential to professional-quality work.

The Crane shot. The cinematographer mounts a *mechanical device that is really a large telescoping arm with the camera attached and a seat for the operator.* The crane allows the camera to *move along a horizontal and a vertical axis.* Since 1930, motorized cranes have permitted the camera to move freely in all directions so that complex movements can be created or followed in space.

Hitchcock arranged a dramatic crane shot in NOTORIOUS where it marks a crucial point in the story. Alexander Sebastian (Claude Rains) gives a party to introduce his bride, Alicia (Ingrid Bergman), to Rio de Janeiro's society. At the beginning of the sequence, the camera located high at the top of the mansion staircase, begins to pan and moves into a high angle extreme long shot of the arriving guests. The camera, mounted on a crane, moves slowly down towards Alicia and Sebastian, who are standing near the front door greeting their guests. Moving closer and closer to the couple, it ends in an extreme close-up of Alicia's hand clutching the key to the wine cellar which she had secretly removed earlier.

The most striking aspect of the shot is that it *moves from an extreme long shot into an extreme close-up without a cut*, all in one fluid motion. Hitchcock, always quite open about the meaning he wanted to establish

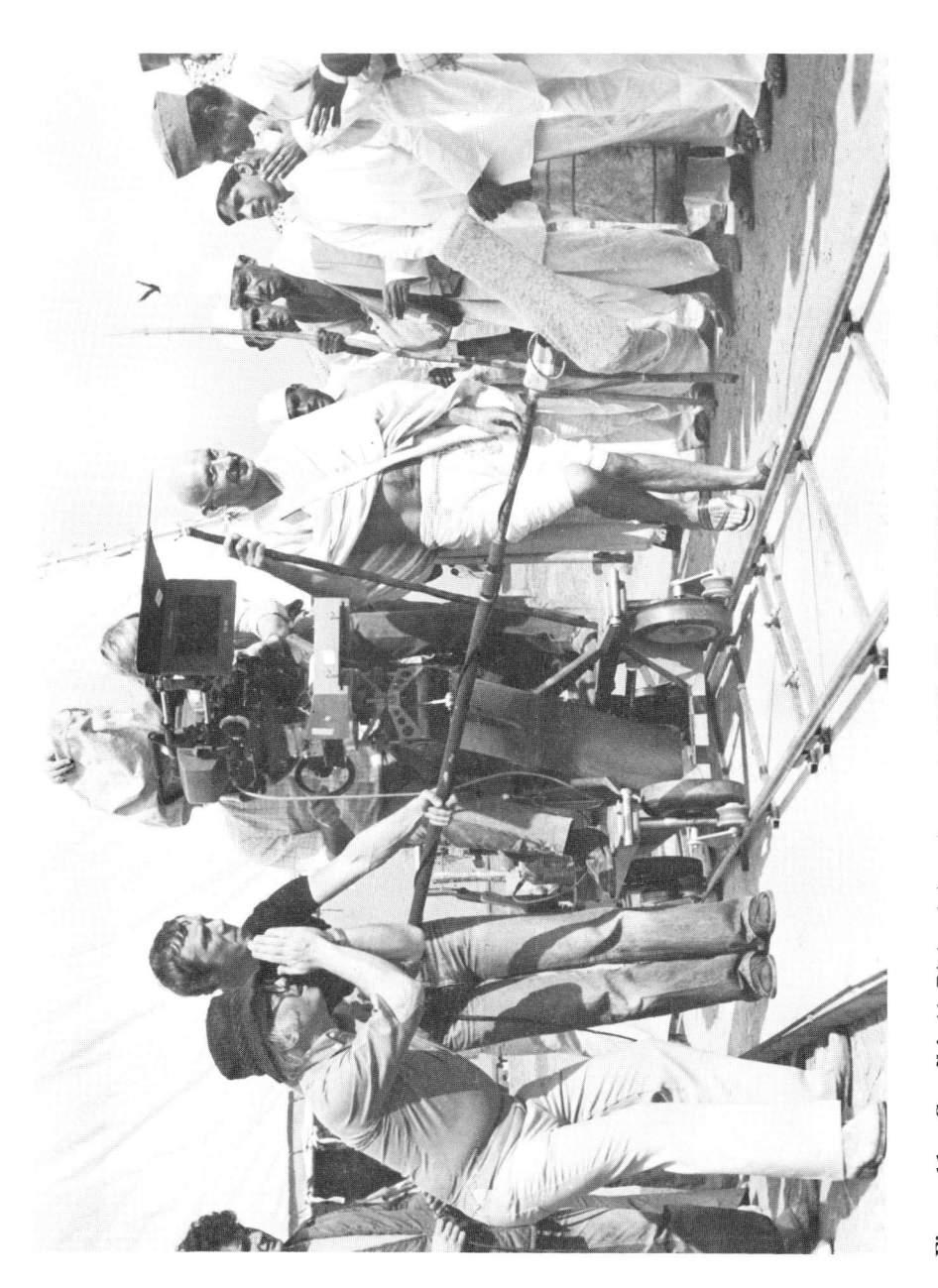

Figure 11. Gandhi (d. Richard Attenborough, 1982). The TRACKING SHOT. Gandhi (Ben Kingsley) walks among his people; the camera accompanies him on tracks laid along his path. The resulting shot will be from Gandhi's point of view. The sound boom is held out of camera range while the director, at left, prompts the crowd.

by his use of shots, stated in an interview with Peter Bogdanovich in *The Cinema of Alfred Hitchcock*, that in this scene a drama was quietly taking place in the midst of a noisy party, in this case a drama centered on a tiny key.

The Dolly shot. *The camera films while mounted on a dolly*, which is like a crane but miniaturized and *equipped with wheels that allow it to move freely*. A simple version has the wheels mounted on a tripod. Because of its smaller size the dolly can go into locations, especially interiors, where the crane would not fit. Originally the dolly was usually used for shorter distances than either the crane or tracks. Nowadays, both dollies and cranes are small, mobil, and flexible and can move through conventional doorways. When mounted on balloon wheels, the dolly produces visually smooth movement. However, filmmakers on low budgets have used everything from a supermarket cart to a wheelchair or a skateboard to capture the results of a dolly.

The Hand-held camera shot. Until recently, professional motion picture cameras were heavy and noisy; consequently hand-held camera shots were nearly impossible. Even filming with a lighter weight, quiet camera, the handheld shot was choppy and hard to watch which limited its use in major commercial films to infrequent times when a director wanted bumpy movement. However, the hand-held camera was widely used by independent filmmakers who appreciated the freedom it gave them.

In the early 1960's, two of the directors of the movement known as the French New Wave, Jean-Luc Godard and Francois Truffaut, making a "virtue of necessity," used lightweight, hand-held cameras in their film debuts, BREATHLESS and THE 400 BLOWS (both 1959), partly because they could not afford expensive dollies. But as young critics who had developed theories on filmmaking and then had become experimental filmmakers, they wanted to rebel against Hollywood's slick style and to produce films that called attention to the camera as well as to the act of filming. They deliberately chose to use the hand-held camera as a way of marking their separateness from the dominant industry and putting their theories into practice.

The success of the New Wave films and the new mobility of the camera brought it to the attention of others who felt a need to break away from Hollywood's confining traditions. In his first film, MEAN STREETS, Martin Scorcese used a constantly moving camera. Many shots in which the camera follows Charlie (Harvey Keitel) are nearly dizzying as it tracks him, hand-held, through apartment hallways, his nightclub hang-out, and along the neighborhood streets, bringing us into the midst of the action.

Italian director Gillo Pontecorvo used a hand-held camera to achieve the look of documentary in THE BATTLE OF ALGIERS which, incidentally, reproduced the experience of being in the midst of the action, jostled by the crowd it was filming.

The camera also produces effects through the filming process by manipulating the lens or the speed of the film. We will mention the most important ones briefly.

In **fast motion** photography, *the camera films at a slower rate than the normal 24 frames per second but the image is projected at normal speed so the action looks speeded up*. **Time-lapse photography** (*the film is shot one frame at a time* allowing a period of time to elapse between each frame) is another way to speed up the motion of normally slow-moving objects such as growing plants and rolling clouds. (See "Special Effects" below.)

Slow motion is the opposite. *The camera films at a faster rate than the normal 24 frames per second but the image is projected at normal speed so the action looks slowed down*. While slow motion used to be "reserved" for dream sequences, in 1967 director Arthur Penn originated another use by showing the deaths of Bonnie and Clyde in very slow motion. It was so effective that it became an expected convention to show death in slow motion.

The Lens/Focal Length/Focus

The **lens** controls the *size, scope, and range of focus*. **Focal length** is *the distance between the lens and the film*. **Focus** is simply *the degree of sharpness of the image*. The choice of lens will affect the look and the meaning of the filmed material. A cameraperson chooses a lens on the basis of its **focal length**, *the distance between the lens and the film mounted in the camera*. The three general categories are the **wide angle, normal**, and **telephoto**.

The **wide angle** requires a *short focal length lens* and produces an image of great *scope*, or breadth. The wide angle lens can keep the image in focus from very close to the camera to "infinity" (as far as the eye can see), but it produces an *optical distortion* that emphasizes an impression of depth. Figures near the camera will be quite large, while things will get smaller very quickly as they move farther away from the camera. These two factors are called **depth of field** (see fig. 12).

The **normal** lens uses a *mid-range focal length* and produces *minimal distortion; it approximates the scope and size of normal vision*. Its range of focus and depth of field are not as great as the wide angle lens so both background and foreground objects can be out of focus. The normal lens is most often used for medium shots (see fig. 6).

The **telephoto** lens has a *long focal length* and produces the opposite effect to that of a wide angle. It has *minimum depth of field*—its range of focus may be no more than a few inches so even slight movement may put the subject out of focus—and it *flattens* the image. Because the telephoto shot is so limited in scope, it may be used for close-ups of wildlife and images that suggest characters being watched. Its narrow range of focus also allows it to emphasize an object by focusing sharply on it and isolating it from its surroundings, kept out of focus.

In further contrast to the wide angle shot, in which a character's progress from background to foreground will seem very rapid, the telephoto shot distorts the sense of distance by making it seem endless and so appears to prevent any progress at all. In the last shot of THE GRADUATE (1967), Dustin Hoffman races against time to get to the church before the woman he loves marries someone else. In a telephoto shot, with the background slightly out of focus, Hoffman, although running frantically, shows great effort and little progress.

The **deep focus shot** requires a *wide angle lens* for *maximum depth of field* and permits the close-up, medium shot, and long shot in focus in the same field. *It allows action in all three planes—the foreground, middleground, and background—to be in focus at the same time* (see fig. 12).

In HOPE AND GLORY (1987), director John Boorman uses a deep focus shot to show a boy returning dejectedly to school, walking along the dark stone wall of the school yard. Framed by the gate, he enters, looks into the schoolyard and sees his schoolmates going wild, cheering, leaping and throwing their books in the air. Behind them is a haze of smoke and dust, the school having been bombed by the Germans. He runs forward, into the action, the kids streaming around him and out the gate in the foreground. The deep focus allows three significant and related pieces of information at once: the boy's reaction in the foreground; the response of the other students in the middleground and background, and the prison-like school buildings in the background.

Focus—*the sharpness of the image*—depends on *selecting the main subject* in the shot and *adjusting the lens* for sharpness and clarity. **Soft focus**, used widely in the 1930's, blurs the image slightly, and was achieved by covering the lens with filters, with gauzy materials, and

Figure 12. The Magnificent Ambersons (d. Orson Welles, 1942). The ballroom of a brilliant set in a deep focus shot. The wide angle lens and strong lighting keep all the planes in focus—from the Christmas tree in close-up at foreground left through the shadowed figures and the rolled-up rug in the mid-foreground, the older couple dancing in the middle ground, to the young couple seated on the stairs in the background. Even the plants and wall lighting fixtures in the extreme background are in sharp focus. The lighted room beyond is at the exact center of the frame, which draws the eye to the vanishing point.

sometimes vaseline. Directors may choose to keep only one area of the framed image sharp or to soften the features of a face.

Rack Focussing or **pulled focus** are terms for the *change of focus during a shot without stopping the camera*. One subject is in focus against an out-of-focus part of the frame. That subject moves out of focus as the focus is "pulled" to bring another subject into focus, usually in the background. Quite common in documentaries and news reports filmed under circumstances that require quick movement from one subject to another and prevent stopping and re-focussing the camera, it is also used in feature films when the director wants to shift attention from a character, or object, or part of the frame to another during the same shot.

The Zoom shot does not actually require camera movement. Rather the lens is designed to shift *focal lengths during the filming without stopping the camera.* The resulting effect (sometimes called "the poor man's dolly shot") gives the impression of moving through space toward or away from a character or object. The zoom can either isolate a figure against out-of-focus surroundings or keep the entire framed image in focus. A fast zoom can be used to create a nearly physical effect in the viewer since it makes space seem to "rush" toward or away from the camera. Hitchcock used a fast zoom for the subjective point of view of Scottie, the main character in VERTIGO (1958). The zoom conveys Scottie's subjective experience, his severe fear of heights: as he looks down, the camera zooms in on the ground below creating the sensation that he and we are plunging downward.

Laboratory Optical Processes

Although laboratory processes are mainly used to produce transitions between sequences and will be discussed as one aspect of editing in Chapter 4, the most common processes that involve the camera are included here for definition. The fade out and fade in are the most common. During a **fade out** the *camera lens opening is gradually closed down, so the image gradually darkens from normal brightness to black.* Occasionally the fade is to another color, for example to white in Mike Nichols's CATCH-22 or to red in Ingmar Bergman's CRIES AND WHISPERS. *The fade out almost always marks the end of a sequence.* During a **fade in** *the camera lens opening is gradually opened so the image gradually brightens from from black (or another color) to normal light. The fade in always marks the beginning of a sequence.*

The **dissolve** (also called a **lap dissolve**, a shortening of "overlapping" dissolve). *One image begins to disappear as another begins to appear so that at a certain point the two images are superimposed upon each other.* The DISSOLVE may be timed to be quick or slow. Very short, quick ones are sometimes used to smooth a cut and are scarcely detectible to the viewer. Long, slow dissolves are used to emphasize the relation between images. Dissolves are often used to introduce a flashback or a dream (see fig. 13).

THE MANCHURIAN CANDIDATE uses the dissolve for both narrative situations. First, Major Marco's nightmare ends with a closeup on

Figure 13. The Gold Rush. Trapped in a cabin by a snowstorm. The Little Tramp's companion, Big Jim McKay, hallucinates from hunger, imagining that the Little Tramp is a chicken. As his vision returns to normal the chicken dissolves back into the Little Tramp.

his face and then a dissolve back to him waking up. The subsequent discussion of the Army's responsibility then dissolves to a black officer, Lieutenant Melvin's nearly identical nightmare (a black version with blacks in the appropriate key roles). Later, when Raymond Shaw tells Marco the story of his meeting and summer romance with Jocelyn Jordan, a long, slow dissolve shows him on the screen telling the story, while the scene of the story comes up slowly in the background.

The **Iris shot** is a type of *masking shot*, in which a part of the image is blocked out, "masked," while another part, usually in the shape of a circle or oval, holds the visible image. "Irising in" and "irising out" describe the contraction and expansion of the image. Commonly used in early silent films, it visually emphasizes a particular point in the frame by closing in on it and then opening to show its relation to the larger setting.

The **freeze frame** (also **freeze shot**) is an optical process in which *a single frame is reprinted many times so that when it is projected it looks like a still photograph*. Francois Truffaut used the freeze for the ending shot of THE 400 BLOWS (1960) in which the young hero, Antoine Doinel (Jean-Pierre Leaud), runs toward the ocean, and as he turns back toward the camera, the shot freezes. Eventually, the freeze became a commonplace way to end films and TV shows.

Special Effects

Some producers in the American film industry believe that realistic filmmaking with its emphasis on location shooting is on the wane and that the future lies in the potential for creating the fantastic locations and science fiction sets that recent advances in computer graphics and special effects technology make possible. The success of new special effects companies—Industrial Light and Magic, the Entertainment Effects Group, and R/Greenberg Associates—tends to support this view. Although most movies continue to be realistic dramas—BROADCAST NEWS, FATAL ATTRACTION, MOONSTRUCK—certainly, there has been an increase in the number of movies that depend on special effects—the STAR WARS series, E.T., *BATTERIES NOT INCLUDED, and others. They have generated a great deal of attention and profits.

Because of the ability of these companies to produce fantastic creatures, distant worlds, and machinery and devices that suggest the far-off future, we may be tempted to think of special effects as a recent phenomenon. Actually, special effects goes back to the beginning of the film business. **Stop motion photography** (also called **pixillation, single frame** or **stop action photography**) is an *animation technique in which the camera shoots one frame at a time while the objects or persons are*

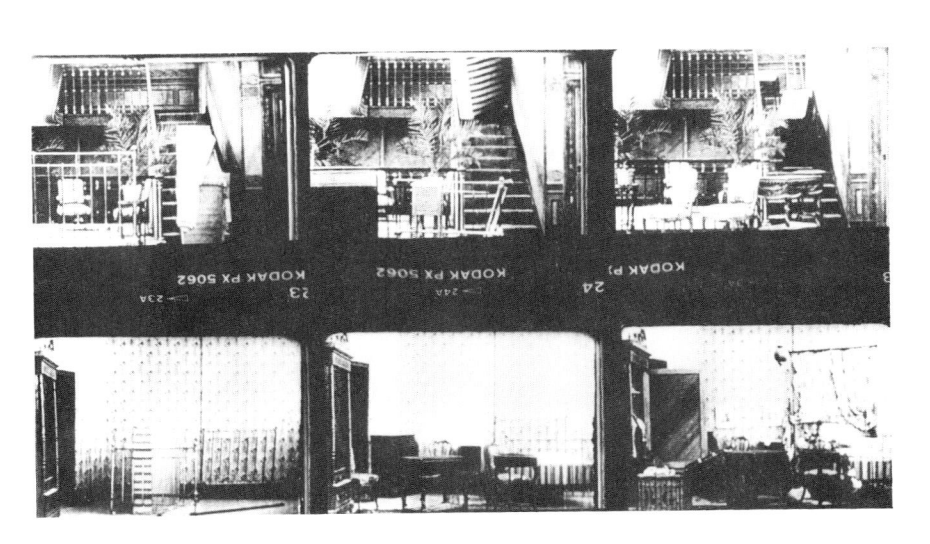

Figure 14. The Automatic Moving Company (d. Emile Cohl, 1910). Selected frames show the magic effect of pixillation as pieces of furniture move themselves upstairs and arrange themselves in a bedroom.

moved a small distance. The first filmmakers, Louis Lumiere and Georges Melies, both used it at the very beginning of the century as did Emil Cohl, who used it to make furniture and other household goods move themselves into a house in his 1910 film, THE AUTOMATIC MOVING COMPANY. Stop motion is the process used in 1933 by the early special effects designer, Willis O'Brien, to make his model of King Kong come alive. It remains useful for the computer-animated action of many of today's screen creatures such as R2D2, C3PO, the extra-terrestrials in STAR WARS, ALIEN, TRON, and of course, E.T.

Another device for producing special effects is called the **Schufftan process**, named after the man who invented it in the 1920's. Eugen Schufftan *constructed a miniature set and reflected it onto a mirror placed close to the camera at a 45 degree angle. Then silver was scraped off places on the back of the mirror; real sets and live actors were placed behind it and the two areas were filmed.* The lighting of the mirror reflection and the real set were so carefully matched that no difference between the two was detectible once the scene was projected onto the screen.

A variation of this process places a painted facsimile or a miniature model close to the camera in such a way that it merges neatly with its surrounding real environment. While this process also dates back to early cinema and is recognizable in films such as THE MAN WHO KNEW TOO MUCH and THE 39 STEPS (both 1935), it was used recently in THE WITCHES OF EASTWICK (1987) for the view of Daryl Van Horne's mansion against the sky.

The **process shot** (also called **rear projection**) is a *projection system in which background, usually scenery, is projected onto a translucent screen while live action takes place in the foreground.* Through this technique, background can be provided without actual location shooting. Hitchcock used rear projection extensively, especially in many scenes where characters drive in cars. VERTIGO, NOTORIOUS, and TO CATCH A THIEF include scenes that use the device to provide backgrounds of California, Florida, and the French Riviera, respectively.

Most special effects processes are extremely time-consuming and very costly. A few minutes on screen might take weeks and cost well over $100,000. The clear advantage is that each animated creature or each element of a laboratory-fabricated environment falls completely under the control of the director.

Some processes are controlled in the laboratory by the use of the **optical printer**. The **matte shot** *prints two separate shots onto a single piece of film stock, resulting in a single image.* In KING KONG it al-

Figure 15. Saving the Proof. The film uses a complex series of travelling mattes to produce visual patterns around a walking figure.

lowed Fay Wray and the gorilla to be seen together in the same frame. The **travelling matte** extends the matte process across several shots. Ray Harryhausen, the animator whose monsters became famous in the 1950's in such films as IT CAME FROM BENEATH THE SEA (1955) and THE SEVENTH VOYAGE OF SINBAD (1959), combined the travelling matte with models using stop motion photography in a process he called "dynamation."

Much matte work (which had become extraordinarily sophisticated even before computers came into common use) depends upon the *rotoscope* and a process called **blue-screen photography**. A chemical response of certain film stocks to blue light makes it possible to film against a blue screen without the image showing.

Figure 16. 2001: A Space Odyssey. This wide-screen frame enlargement illustrates the use of the blue-screen process to create a view of outer space.

    These techniques have been supplemented, if not supplanted, recently by video and computer techniques which offer increased possibilities to the filmmakers who have the means to do the "impossible." At the same time, the artistry of these techniques makes it difficult for viewers to "see" the effects because even the most fantastic ones "look so real." The vivid imaginary worlds of STAR WARS, creatures like E.T., and incredible feats like the light-saber fight of STAR WARS and the flying bicycle trip at the end of E.T., created in the laboratory, are so "life-like" that they seem magical. The creation of special effects is only one of the many ways in which the movies fascinate and manipulate us. All the techniques discussed in this chapter make up the "vocabulary" available to filmmakers. The next chapters will attempt to define and clarify strategies in which the processes are used.

CHAPTER 3
Scene and Subject

We all know that without a camera there would be no movie. The cinema, first and foremost, requires the camera. But the camera is only a single element in the complex technology that produces finished films. It also calls for sophisticated lights, sound equipment, editing equipment, laboratory facilities, and projection capabilities. Yet equipment only makes the process of filming possible; cameras must always film *something*.

As we saw in the preceding chapter, even special effects and optical effects, which create beings, events and meanings that don't exist in everyday reality, must be *constructed as models, graphic images, or reworked images* before they can be filmed. In our examination of movies, it makes sense to consider what we actually see when we watch a movie; in this chapter we will concentrate on *what is in front of the camera, people in action on location*—the **scene** and the **subject**.

But first let us consider the division of responsibility in a film production. Every movie requires a **producer, a writer, a director, a cinematographer, an editor, and a distributor**. Sometimes one person functions in more than one capacity but the work is essential and must be carried out. The producer and the writer usually figure primarily in the *pre-production* stage of the film, that is, in *the developmental stages* before any filming is done. The **producer** acquires the script, chooses a director, cast, and crew, assures financial backing, and determines locations. After these preliminary arrangements have been worked out, the producer's job is to oversee the progress of the whole production through to its completion and distribution.

The **director** takes charge of the *production* stage, supervising the cinematographer, the set designers, the actors, and the sound and lighting crews. The director also works with the writer and producer during the pre-production phase. In fact many successful Hollywood directors have been deeply involved in both writing and producing: Alfred Hitchcock, George Lucas, and Francis Coppola, to name just a few. Independent filmmakers, because they work on lower budgets and especially because their films are often very personal conceptions, are usually active in all phases of their films. John Sayles, Jim Jarmush, documentary filmmakers, Judy Irving and Chris Beaver, Pat Ferrero, David and Judith MacDougall, and Trinh T. Minh-ha write, direct, and often film and edit their own work.

The final stage, *post-production, readies the film for release*. During this stage the picture is edited, the sound track is scored and edited, and all optical and special effects work is completed. While the director usually supervises this stage, in industry productions the producer retains the right to override the director's decisions.

In most cases, the director works with both the writer and the producer during the pre-production stage and with the writer throughout the whole production so that they may make necessary revisions during filming. But the production stage is essentially under the director's personal control. S/he supervises three crucial areas: cinematography and lighting; acting, costume and make-up; set design. Each of these areas requires its own crew of specialists and assistants. The **director of photography**, or **cinematographer**, works with the director on the selection of framing and set-ups and directs the highly complicated lighting arrangements for each shot. The **art director**, or **set designer**, oversees researchers, artists, and a crew of carpenters and decorators. Finally, the director works with the actors who are, in turn, supported by specialists in costuming and make-up.

Scene

The word **scene** comes to film from the theatre where it means both a specific place on a stage ("the scene was Venice") and the events that occur there in a continuous segment of time ("the scene of Hamlet's soliloquy"). Strictly speaking, in film the term is also used to refer to a **sequence** in which the *action takes place in a single place and time*. But movies are made up of many story fragments, so many sequences do not take place in a single location; a "scene" is only one way of developing action. In film many scenes involve gaps in time and more than one location. Our concern here is with *scene* as it is created in front of the camera.

Mise en scene (pronounced "meez on sen") when translated from French, means *placement into the scene* or, in everyday English, "setting the scene," and is another phrase borrowed by film from the theatre. The term covers *the organization of everything that is put in front of the camera in preparation for filming* and, most importantly, *the way those*

Figure 17. Gone with the Wind (d. Victor Fleming, 1939). The "mise en scene" for a complicated shot on the staircase.

things are arranged to create a dramatically and aesthetically appealing composition—sets; lighting; actors and their actions, their costumes, and their make-up. Wide screen production requires directors to pay strict attention to *mise en scene* because it emphasizes location of characters and action (see fig. 17).

Let us look at the way *mise en scene* places elements in front of the camera.

The Set

Sets are the *"little worlds" created in the production studio*. Studios use *sound-stages*, large spaces planned for good acoustics and good lighting, in which the set designers plan and construct the **decors**. Some studios also have exterior studio space where special outdoor environments, such as a town of "the Old West," can be fabricated. Nowadays sets are built and maintained in several areas of the United States for television productions.

Figure 18. How Green Was My Valley (d. John Ford, 1941). The "little world," a romantic Ireland created in the production studio.

The set can be seen as a frame for the movements of both actors and camera. The camera must be able to move around a set, passing from room to room, climbing stairs, circling freely in a ballroom, hovering high above the action, or taking the place of characters within the action (see fig. 12). Because the camera records details so precisely and because the film industry is, at least in the United States, committed to the production of realistic fiction, the set designers—experts in the construction of a believable world large enough in its dimensions to allow camera and actors into it—have had to "recreate reality."

Since the cost of set design and construction is very high, directors work with the designers to plan out production requirements before a final shooting script has even been completed. Designers, the director, and the producer discuss the costs of labor and materials and, after researching the appropriate decor and architecture, the designer sketches each scene.

Set design and construction are never a small operation. The designer must supervise a crew: a research assistant, a light and color specialist, a costume designer. In addition a production that uses a sound stage requires a store of furniture and ready access to carpenters, metalworkers, painters, electricians, and decorators. A commercially produced feature may take anywhere from fifty to two hundred skilled craftspersons and technical, artistic, even military advisers have been consulted by designers to ensure authenticity of the set.

Blocking/Choreography

Blocking and **choreography** are terms for *plotting the movements of camera and actors.* The ability to visualize the movements of actors as they interact with the camera (itself often also moving) is essential to the task of both the director and the set designer, who must be able to create a set not for just a couple of shots but for the whole film (see fig. 17). Alfred Hitchcock's film, ROPE (1948), was shot in a single location with hardly any detectable cutting and a camera that followed the actors all over a set that was made up of at least three rooms. It was the job of the set designer to make sure that the decor in all three rooms was realistic and "worked," and that there was ample space to **block**—that is, *plan* or *"choreograph" the movement of camera and actors* (see fig. 52).

Orson Welles's THE MAGNIFICENT AMBERSONS (1942), demanded the creation of a very elaborate set since the location was supposed to be the mansion of a very wealthy family. The ballroom sequence alone required space that would allow the camera and the two main couples, dancing, to interact in relation to one another (see fig. 12).

The choice and placement of **props**—*furniture, upholstery, decoration*, all the various pertinent objects of the decor—are vital to the significance of a scene and must be carefully considered. At times the director has emphasized a set so heavily that it seems to take on significance beyond that of background to the action. Josef von Sternberg's *mise en scene* is highly textured; he crowds the sets with objects and emphasizes them with dramatic lighting. The sets of BLADE RUNNER (1982) are oppressive and claustrophobic, a labyrinth of gigantic electronic billboards, squalid, narrow, overcrowded streets, dank warehouses, and over-sized skyscrapers—all created in the special effects lab. For MISHIMA (1985) Paul Schrader used detailed and expressionistic sets inter-cut with everyday realistic scenes to make a statement about the complex psychology of the writer-philosopher, Yukio Mishima, the subject of the story while at the same time conveying a sense of the man's writings (see fig. 44).

Location

The **location** is an *actual place that serves as the backdrop for the action* and is not, of course, controllable the way a set constructed especially for the film is. Shooting on location goes back to 1895 when Lumiere set up his camera in his garden, outside his factory, and at the seashore to record "scenes of everyday life." Since then, location shooting has been important in the fiction film where it must contribute to the realistic and dramatic effects of the story or to the *genre*; it is, of course, the only place for the production of documentaries.

For a long time the problems of producing good quality sound, coupled with the bulkiness of production equipment, made location shooting difficult. However, some types of films that required natural settings, in particular adventure stories and westerns, were always filmed at least partly on location in places like Lone Pine in Eastern California, or Arizona, or Monument Valley, Utah, or the Hollywood backlots. Since the 1960's, because of the development of lightweight sound cameras, tape recorders, and lighting equipment, theatrical release films have been able to "take to the hills" as well as to the streets as much as they wish.

In general, locations are carefully chosen both for the "feel" of the place and to contribute to the meaning of the film. For example, in VERTIGO (1958) Alfred Hitchcock filmed in San Francisco and the surround-

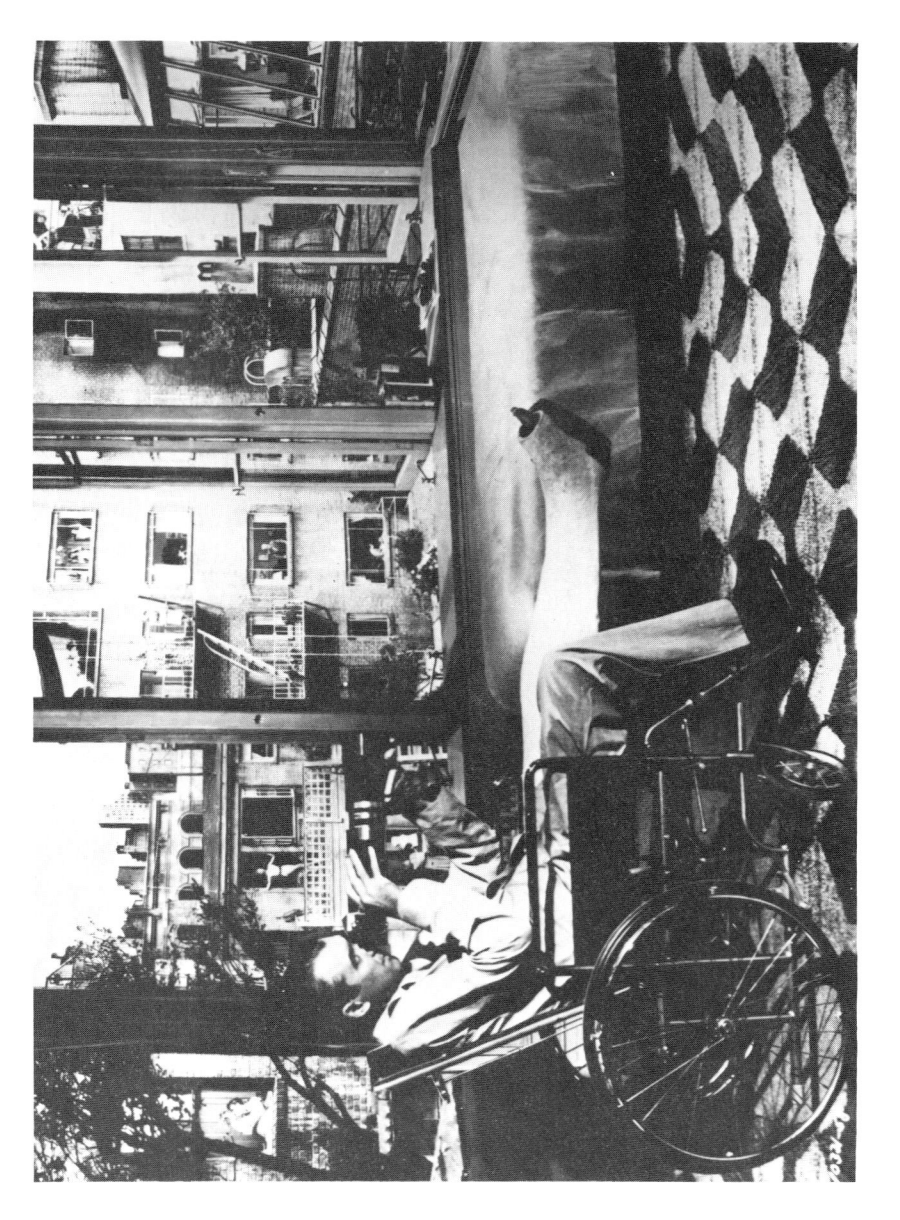

Figure 19. Rear Window (d. Alfred Hitchcock 1954). The mise en scene reveals Jeff's (James Stewart) voyeurism when, confined by a broken leg, this professional photographer focuses his camera before turning it towards his neighbors. The set, with its props and decor and the positions of the other characters in their windows, make up the little world of the film.

Figure 20. Movie Flat, Lone Pine, CA. A commonly used location until the 1940's. Gunga Din, The Ox-Bow Incident and later, How The West Was Won, were all shot in this area.

ing Bay Area. He deliberately set out to demonstrate that bright daylight, stunning natural landscapes, and a pastel-colored city could conceal murder, deceit, corruption, and despair as much as the dark and harsh urban settings of the thrillers of the late 1940's.

The development of any film story depends upon location. Imagine a situation in which the hero is being chased by a villain. Put the characters on horses in a desert setting, give them Winchester rifles, and you have a western (THE SEARCHERS, 1956; SILVERADO, 1985). Put them into 1930's automobiles in an urban setting, give them machine guns and 38's, and you have a gangster movie (SCARFACE, 1932; BONNIE AND CLYDE, 1969; THE UNTOUCHABLES, 1987; THE GODFATHER, 1972; ONCE UPON A TIME IN AMERICA, 1984). Put the main character in a beat up Honda and the villains in a dark gray-green Chevrolet, make the weapon radiation contamination, and you have a contemporary realistic drama (SILKWOOD, 1983). Put them in a futuristic

Figure 21. In one interview published in *Focus on Hitchcock*, the director described the convention he wanted to avoid in his own films: the protagonist is placed "under the street lamp at night in a pool of light, waiting, very sinister surroundings, the cobbles are all washed by the recent rain. . . ." The strong contrasts between light and shadow are also typical of the "film noir."

space ship, give them light-sabres, and you have, of course, science fiction (STAR WARS, 1977). (The issue is also connected to the organization of "genre," and will be discussed from that perspective in chapter 6.)

Although they impose different restrictions and offer different possibilities to the director, the set and the location must fulfill all essential needs of the production. On the one hand they must provide all the scenery required by the story—furniture, decor, buildings, landscapes. But they must also eliminate any *inappropriate* elements, out-of-period traces such as onlookers, jet trails, high power lines, and any others that threaten to undermine the believability of the world created on the screen. Some filmmakers even transform or modify natural locations for purposes of story and style.

It is the job of the **continuity assistant** to *ensure visual consistency* in the film. But a discrepancy in a scene, an incongruous or anachronistic element, may be included for humor, political emphasis, or for experimentation. Jean-Marie Straub and Danielle Huillet in HISTORY

Figure 22. Blazing Saddles (d. Mel Brooks, 1974). The Sheriff rides through the "Old West" and comes upon Count Basie and his jazz band.

LESSONS (1972) introduce a man wearing an ancient roman toga into modern day Rome to make a political connection between the two periods. Mel Brooks in BLAZING SADDLES (1974), inserts contemporary elements like modern popular songs and references into "the early West" to parody the western.

Color

The director and the set designer also must consider whether to use **black/white/gray** or full **color** cinematography; each has its own powerful photographic and thematic significance and a different effect on audiences. in the past, economic considerations have had some bearing on the decision but for today, for the most part, color is in common use and industry directors must work within the constraints of the "state of the art" in photography as in all other areas of film technology.

Nowadays we take the "fact" of color in a film for granted because we are accustomed to it as so much a part of our regular filmgoing experience. If the film is meant to be realistic, color will not be a noticeable part of the experience. But some filmmakers, aware of the way movies actually change our view of the world, often manipulate color in more or less subtle ways so as to force us to notice it, or to see it "differently." At that point, color becomes an element of art and meaning.

In the 1920's, the Soviet director Sergei Eisenstein recognized that colors have traditional and/or cultural meaning: in his country, red is identified with rage, pink with passion, blue with cold, and black with death. (In China, red is a color of joy and luck and white is for funerals.) Eisenstein was able to apply his hypotheses to actual practice with dramatic results in several sequences of IVAN THE TERRIBLE (1944) which he shot in color leaving the rest in black and white.

Directors and cinematographers have continued to be interested in color and the way it can influence the viewer. Some have used it in an expressive or symbolic way; Vittorio Storaro, the cinematographer of THE LAST EMPEROR, researched colors and their psychoanalytic associations. In an interview published in *Masters of Light* (Ed. Schaefer and Salvato, 1984), he discussed his intention to relate characters to colors that express their personality. He carried out this experiment in the theory of color symbolism in Bernardo Bertolucci's LUNA (1979) and Francis Coppola's ONE FROM THE HEART (1982).

Ingmar Bergman developed highly complex symbolic relationships in his use of black and white cinematography in his early films, especially

Figure 23. The Seventh Seal (d. Ingmar Bergman, 1956). Black and white tonals mark the contrast between the two figures. The knight plays chess with Death for his life. The faces are perfectly contrasted against the sky; the knight's head is in shadow leaving his face and head outlined in light, paralleling Death's face outlined by the black hood. The chess board, an important element in the frame, is lit dramatically.

THE SEVENTH SEAL (1956) (see fig. 23), THE VIRGIN SPRING (1959), and WILD STRAWBERRIES (1957). He created dramatic tonal qualities and went on to work in an equally complex way with color. For the transitions between scenes in CRIES AND WHISPERS (1972), he used dissolves to *red* and red walls for the set that together create a persistent and oppressive motif of blood, passion, and torment. In FANNY AND ALEXANDER (1963), just the opposite—soft pastels—evoke romantic childhood memories.

Any discussion of color must mention Michelangelo Antonioni's early experiment in his first color film RED DESERT (1964). He distorted natural colors to produce the effect of an unnatural world, meant to be a reflection of the main character's mental anguish. He had a street vendor's fruit tinted gray, a waterfront shack painted a brilliant red, and captured images of the yellow, polluted smoke billowing from a factory. The harsh primary colors in contrast to grayed down colors of the rest of the scene depict the character's intense anxiety.

Black and white cinematography is a significant part of the experience of watching a film such as CITIZEN KANE, DOUBLE INDEMNITY, THE SEVENTH SEAL, THE RULES OF THE GAME; similarly, color is meaningful in films such as the two parts of THE GODFATHER (1972 and 1974), CHINATOWN (1974), and MISHIMA (1985).

Lighting

Without a camera there can be no movie; but, in the most basic terms, *without light there can be no image. The picture is, finally, only light—patterns of light and dark, projected on a flat, two-dimensional surface—the screen in the theatre.* Anyone who has ever used a non-automatic, still camera knows how easy it is to **under-expose**, that is, *allow too little light* onto the film stock, or **over-expose**, *allow too much light*. A photograph taken at the beach, if not carefully controlled may turn out nearly white because the intense glare of reflected sunlight over-exposes the film.

During a film production, whether on a set or location, lighting, the job of the cinematographer of director of photography, the D.P., can take many hours. The **choice of lighting**, is a *function of camera placement;* in fact, a simple change of camera angle will almost always require a completely new lighting set-up. The lights are placed and adjusted by a skilled crew of lighting technicians, called **gaffers**. They work under the supervision of the cinematographer, whose extensive technical knowledge of the camera, film stocks, and lighting makes it possible to create the proper effects.

A Historical Note

During the 1920's, German Expressionism emerged as a movement in art, theater, and film. The Expressionist filmmakers, aware of the symbolism in the play of light and shadow, even painted shadows on their sets. The movement became noted especially for its use of contrasting lighting. In the 1930's and '40's, lighting became defined by the style of directors. For his star actress, Marlene Dietrich, Joseph von Sternberg insisted on lighting that modeled her face and emphasized her stylized pos-

Figure 24. Double Indemnity (d. Billy Wilder, 1944). Classic example of "film noir" lighting. Fred McMurray and Barbara Stanwyck discuss "insurance" in a room full of shadows and pools of darkness. The bleak mood of the lighting reflected the film's themes of corruption and despair.

tures. In BLONDE VENUS and SHANGHAI EXPRESS (both 1932), Dietrich's face is often half-hidden by shadows, hat brims, beads, and gauzy curtains. At the other extreme, Orson Welles, resisted the trend to diffuse light and required the intense lighting necessary for sharply focussed composition in depth. The contrasts that result underline the mood of the films and the complexity of character.

French film critics writing during the '50's for the film journal, *Cahiers du cinema* ("Cinema Notebooks"), looking back at the grim, tough, detective films and thrillers of the late 1940's, named them *film noir*, or "dark film," because of the somber themes, black and white photography, and contrasting lighting which the critics noted were the films' stylistic trademark. In the "noir" films (DOUBLE INDEMNITY, 1944; THE BIG SLEEP, 1946; THE POSTMAN ALWAYS RINGS

Figure 25. The Postman Always Rings Twice (d. Tay Garnett, 1946). The light casts shadows of unseen cell bars emphasizing the idea of a moral and physical cage in which this man is trapped. Like Figure 24, the film noir mood of the lighting is bleak and despairing.

TWICE, 1946; OUT OF THE PAST, 1947; among others), the intense contrast between light and dark in combination with the other elements suggest the hidden dangers of a corrupt and violent world and create a bleak and pessimistic mood (see figs. 21, 24, 25, 36). "Noir" lighting continues to be so recognizable today that parodies and homages depend specifically on reproducing the lighting.

The Technique of Lighting

The technique of lighting consists of working with the **contrast ratio** *between darker and lighter portions* of the set. **Film stocks** have different **tolerances** for contrast, so the cinematographer has to be sure that the *range between the darkest and lightest areas* of the set or location is *not too extreme* for the film type being used. Then the cinematographer, working with lights of varying intensities, must **model** the scene *to bring out or emphasize the characters and shapes of objects* that most effectively convey the meaning the director intends to establish through the shot.

The independent director John Sayles, in his book *Thinking In Pictures,* describes the lighting strategy he used in his film MATEWAN (1987). For this story of coal miners in the 1920's, Sayles and his cinematographer, Haskell Wexler, wanted to avoid conventional lighting set-ups for the shots inside the mines. Miners of that period worked using low-intensity, carbide headlamps, inadequate, of course, for filming. Sayles wanted the scenes to show the real darkness in which the miners worked but their activities had to be visible on the screen. Wexler solved the problem by setting up what he called a "diffuse spotlight." He carefully aimed it *past* the miner without focussing on any one spot and, at the same time, moved it "in sync" with the miner's head to make it appear to be coming from the headlamp. The set-up was so complex that the least slip in timing would ruin the shot.

The single-light set-up used for MATEWAN is rare; most productions use many lights. Just a basic lighting set-up involves **key** lights, the *primary* or *key* source of illumination; **fill** lights, that reduce the contrast between the light and dark areas and *fill in between the key lights,* modify the formation of pools of light and darkness because they are generally softer, diffuse, and of lower intensity than the key light; and quite often, **backlights** which, as the name suggests, are *placed behind the subject and separate it from the background.* While not part of the basic set-up, the **bounce** light is common both in studios and on location. It reflects or bounces intense light off a bright white wall or a metallic reflector; this *reduces the strength of the light and diffuses it over the area to be photographed.* Other optional lights are **hairlights** which get their name because they are a *small spot-light* placed high behind the subject which illuminates the hair and the back of the head creating a halo effect. **Kickers** are placed near the feet, at floor level, aimed upward and also serve to *separate subject from background.*

The position of the key light is determined by the kind of emphasis and mood the director wants to achieve, and the location of any **motivated** source of light, which *appears to emerge from a real source—* a lamp on a table or sun streaming in a window. A shot that involves movement of the actors or of the camera from one spot to another requires more than one key light. A long shot or a deep focus shot may in-

Figure 26. Citizen Kane. Rich lighting "motivated" by the table lamp provides brilliant white areas, calling attention to Kane's idealistic "Statement of Principles." The low angle on Kane is balanced by the eye level shots on Bernstein and Leland.

volve several key lights for strong illumination in different areas of the set (see fig. 26).

The cinematographer and the director make decisions on lighting according to the demands of the particular film because, besides being essential to image, lighting is also crucial to the production of meaning. Vittorio Storaro (APOCALYPSE NOW (1979), THE LAST TANGO IN PARIS (1973), THE LAST EMPEROR (1987) has said in an interview that he considers the cinematographer to be like a writer and filming to be like writing with light that enables the viewer to feel and understand, both consciously and unconsciously, the meaning of the story.

If the lighting is not flamboyant, or dramatic, or striking, it will not be noticed at all—as "lighting." The drive for realism, even in nonrealistic genres like science fiction, restricts experimentation and any obvious manipulation of lighting. Nevertheless, many directors have used it to add effect and meaning to their films.

Subject

Actors and Acting

The locations, sets, decors—the scene—are the backdrop for the **subject:** *people.* In documentaries the subject is most likely to be *real* people, filmed either in interviews or life situations. But because of the tradition and popularity of fiction films (and the power of the entertainment industry), actors have been most strongly associated with the movies, although recently the director has begun to share in the recognition usually reserved for stars. But to most people, actors, the stars *are* movies. They, more than any others in the filmmaking process, elicit audience response and that response can be either sympathy or dislike, it doesn't seem to matter which. In the 1920's, Erich von Stroheim was advertised as "the man you love to hate," and he attracted a strong following; these days, Larry Hagman—J.R. of course—has inherited his position.

A great deal of money is at stake in every film production. And just as advertising sells its products by depending on quick recognition of a product logo, films also depend on recognition of a "logo"—the movie star. People go to an "Eddie Murphy film" or "see everything" that

Figure 27. The Blue Angel (d. Josef von Sternberg, 1931). Marlene Dietrich's role in this film brought her to the attention of the American movie public. Along with Garbo she went on to become one of Hollywood's most compelling female stars.

Meryl Streep has made, just as in the early days of the movies, adoring fans turned out specially for the films of Charlie Chaplin, Greta Garbo, and Gary Cooper. Hollywood (like the television industry) tries hard to build stars out of the actors so that loyal fans will always be available.

The physical appearance of the actors is taken into consideration in the making of the film because appearance is another element that imparts meaning. Actors are chosen for their "look," which becomes part of what is called **iconography**, which in this case is *the likeness or image of the actor which produces a particular meaning.* As an example, when we think of John Wayne, one of the best known actors ever to come out of the "star system," we think of a specific range of meanings and connotations associated with him, inseparable from the roles and characters he played: John Wayne over the years came to represent ruggedness, courage, integrity, and masculine authority. Among contemporary actors, Jack Nicholson has combined boyishness with the devilish charm of a smooth, fast-talking operator in such films as CHINATOWN (1974),

Figure 28. The Left Handed Gun (d. Arthur Penn, 1958). Paul Newman did not yet have the star status that he currently holds. The actor's strong, unwavering gaze is characteristic of the western hero.

TERMS OF ENDEARMENT (1983), PRIZZI'S HONOR (1985). Among actresses, Jane Fonda combines the conventional requirements of feminine good looks with a more contemporary independence and strength of character and resourcefulness in JULIA (1977), COMING HOME (1978), CHINA SYNDROME (1979), ON GOLDEN POND (1981). In addition, largely because of emotional associations, "beloved" stars, like Paul Newman or Robert Redford, can "make" a picture, that is, make it successful, just by agreeing to appear in it.

Screen Acting

The difference between theatrical acting and film acting is that on the stage, acting is expansive whereas on the screen it tends to be more subtle. The reason for the difference is fairly obvious. In the theatre the audience is always relatively far away from the actors who must *project* their voices, gestures, and actions, so that all the spectators, whether seated in the first row of the orchestra or in the last row of the balcony, can grasp the play. Incidentally, that is why the acting in silent films,

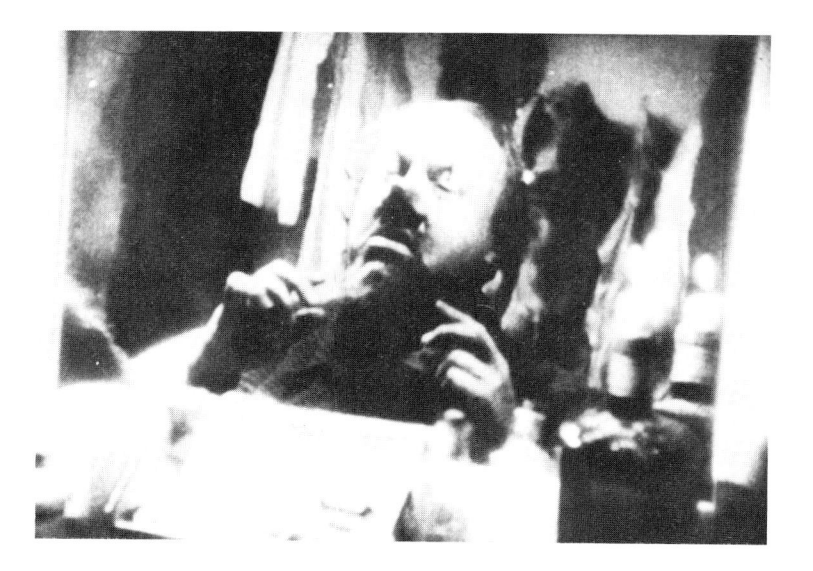

Figure 29. The Blue Angel. Emil Jannings (Professor Rath in the film) makes himself up to go on-stage in the Blue Angel cabaret. Although Jannings' screen acting style is "theatrical" by current standards, his performance, here in medium shot, would have been impossible on the stage because it depends entirely on expression and small gestures of the head and hands.

which had to rely on gesture rather than words, immediately strikes contemporary viewers as "theatrical"— exaggerated and hammy.

Once directors realized that the camera was free to move close to the actors, they saw that the close-up would reveal even the most intense emotions. The slightest tightening around the lips, a glance, the slow clenching of a fist or stiffening of the shoulders, magnified by the close-up, will express meaning and emotion even more powerfully than a large gesture. Because of the physical presence of the camera and because of editing (which we shall examine in the next chapter), film acting is more complex technically than stage acting where each performance takes place in one continuous, real, time period, regardless of dramatic time. A film is composed of hundreds of shots, each of which must be acted separately and films are shot, not in the chronological order of the story, but according to the time of day, the season, and the place of the action (interiors, exteriors, on location, on a studio set). Shots that follow one another directly in the finished film may have been filmed days, weeks, even months apart. Film actors may not have to memorize lines like their theatrical counterparts do, but they have to step into their roles every time there is a new take or a new shot.

The actors must also work not only with each other but also with a camera which is usually moving. The director diagrams the **blocking**, that is, *the movements of both actors and camera*, to bring both to the right place at precisely the right time. The difficulties this may involve are illustrated in descriptions of the filming of Alfred Hitchcock's UNDER CAPRICORN (1949). The shots were nearly ten minutes long; the camera was in constant motion, moving about the set, dollying in for a close-up on one actor, then circling away to concentrate on another. The performers were also in constant movement and had to search for and arrive at their place markers on the floor at the exact moment they were to be filmed. The slightest lapse in timing or a missed destination meant redoing the entire take. Ingrid Bergman, the star, was supposed to have broken down under the stress.

Conclusion

Making a film is a complex undertaking. A convincing set is created by specialists according to the specifications of the director and the producer and must accommodate the camera and actors. Lighting, which literally and figuratively illuminates the set and the action, and often adds a separate level of meaning, must be determined and controlled. The actors must perform and maintain their roles from one shot to the next. Everything that takes place in front of the camera must be carefully planned through all the phases from writing the script to shooting the action; all significant information, from concrete details to the most subtle levels of thematic suggestion, must be captured in the images on the screen.

Looking at the films it is hard to imagine that the fluid events we see on the screen were once many fragments, filmed at different times and in different places and later transformed into continuous action on the editor's bench, like scraps of fabric stitched into a patchwork quilt. By the time the film reaches the theatre screen all traces of difficulty have been erased and the most amazing feats look easy, natural, graceful, and refined. In the next chapter we will examine the process that achieves that transformation into the film we eventually see in the theatre—editing.

CHAPTER 4
Editing

Editing is the single most important element in the creation of a movie. As we have seen, camera angle, distance, lighting and many other elements contribute to the finished film but editing is crucial. The editor must take all the filmed material and *arrange* it. By *juxtaposing the pieces of film—putting them next to each other in a specific order*— editing organizes the bits of meaning in each single shot into sequences, and finally into a coherent work. In this chapter we will explain how editing is done, why it is important, and just how it creates meaning in movies.

A Historical Note

When filmmakers first began to make movies back around the turn of this century, they did not edit: they just aimed the camera and shot until the film ran out. The filmmaker would set the shot up far enough away from the action to get it all into the frame. As a result, the camera was like the spectator in a theater, seated in the orchestra center, viewing the whole stage, with characters entering and leaving the scene, from that one vantage point. Short skits , "gags," and "playlets" that could be staged over the short time before the film ran out were recorded and projected. In fact, the movies borrowed its ideas and terminology from the theatre. The words "scene," "set," "decor," "producer," "director," found their way into the vocabulary of the new medium.

By 1901, several pioneer film directors had begun to string shots together, creating scenes that were long enough to develop action. They recognized the medium's potential for telling stories that needed more than one location. Now the spectator could see scenes of several different locations in the same film but s/he was still stuck in Row M Center watching the action in long shot. About ten years later, D. W. Griffith began to explore the *expressive power* of the close-up and the medium shot and "interrupted" the action from time to time, to **cut in** to a close-up of a character's emotion-filled face. *Cutting in and away from shots* became standard procedure and continues to be the basis of most editing today.

Once directors recognized the enormous flexibility editing gave them, they came to think of filmmaking as something like writing, with its own "grammar," the camera as a pen, and the director as a writer using it. They considered that the arrangement of shots into scenes, and scenes into sequences was like putting words together into paragraphs and chapters. And in fact, just as writers edit by actually cutting up sentences and paragraphs and rearranging them, film editing always requires deletions, re-phrasing, re-organization.

People who have experience with a word processor know how easy it is to rearrange material and how each arrangement affects both the ideas and the meaning of what is written. In many ways editing film is the same. The filmmaker, like the writer, must decide what material will be used and in what order. As in writing, film editing is not limited to just assembling and reassembling bits of information in pictures; just like writing which is governed by principles of grammar and construction, film editing developed standards and conventions. And just as editing is a powerful tool in writing, its power in film soon became apparent.

The movies never dropped the terms it borrowed from theatre and writing nor the concepts they describe, but as directors began to use techniques only the camera was capable of, the cinema evolved its own rather descriptive vocabulary, one that was specific to its technology.

Making the Film

Experienced directors of any kind of film—fiction, documentary, or experimental—often begin work with a written proposal, a "treatment," a script or screenplay, a storyboard or shooting script. In narrative films a script defines the characters, plot, dramatic action, whereas a **storyboard** is more often used in documentaries and alternative cinema and is a *visualization of the film*. The filmmaker *sketches an idea of the way the shots should look and plans the set-ups in preparation for the filming*, called the **shoot**.

With or without a storyboard, many filmmakers edit while filming by pre-selecting shots or by stopping the camera for periods when the action is not to be recorded. But in fiction films, the filmmaker usually shoots several set-ups (the combination of camera angle, distance, and lighting) in several **takes**, *the recording of a shot on film*. In documentaries it is often impossible to re-shoot, so a great deal of material is shot that will be cut out and thrown away. This is a real difference between making a fiction film and making a documentary film, but in almost all other ways the activity of assembling a film is the same for all types of movies.

As the filming progresses, the director selects the best take of each shot on the basis of **rushes** or **dailies**, *the footage shot each day*. Then the editor, working with the director or according to plan, puts together a **rough cut** on a **work print**, which, like a "rough draft" of a paper, can be scratched and changed, cut and pasted. By this point the editor has laid out the main lines of the film and has synchronized the sound with the images. Then s/he makes a **fine cut**, still on the work print, as *close to the final form of the film* as possible. After *music and sound effects* are added in a process called **mixing** where *recorded tracks of all the sounds* (from two or three to more than a hundred) *are blended electronically*, the **original print** is **conformed** to the work print. *Conforming the original means that it is cut and arranged exactly in the same order as the work print* has been. Finally, the original is sent to the laboratory where **titles** are added and finally, **release prints** are made which go out to the theaters.

The Shooting Ratio

Directorial style, methods of filming, the type of film—documentary or fiction or a particular genre (western, thriller, musical, etc.)—require different approaches to editing. Various factors determine the number of times the shot or scene will have to be filmed and *that number determines the amount of material that will be processed through the editing*. The **shooting ratio**, the *amount of film footage that is finally used in proportion to the amount that is discarded*, varies as a result of all of these factors. At one extreme, documentary filmmakers Judy Irving and Chris Beaver, who went out to "get the story" for DARK CIRCLE (1983), a film on nuclear proliferation, shot 20 times more footage than they finally used in the finished film. At the other extreme, Alfred Hitchcock prepared each film so carefully beforehand that very little footage was discarded and editing was a relatively small part of his filmmaking process.

Cutting: A Description

How exactly is editing accomplished? It is actually done by *cutting* up the film stock and pasting the pieces together. The editor places a strip of film on a splicer, a machine that holds it in place by its sprocket holes; then s/he selects and marks a specific frame and cuts with the razor-sharp blade which is a part of the splicer. S/he either tapes or hot-splices (cements under heat) one piece to the next so that different shots are attached to each other. The editor separates—cuts—each shot from its original material and attaches it to other shots. Once the editor has made decisions about grouping the shots— conventionally, these are based on such factors as unity of time and location, the quality of the take—s/he assembles them into **sequences**, *the first definable action meaningful in itself.* And, just as in writing, *differing arrangements within each sequence and between the sequences can change the meaning of the whole film.*

Classical Editing

As we have said, the basic unit of construction in film is the shot. The single shot is connected to others to form sequences that are internally coherent. The sequences are then connected to one another to form the whole film. Through complex relationships between sequences, the film tells the story or conveys information. The classical Hollywood cinema developed as a story-telling medium and like the popular novel, films tried to make the story flow smoothly, "seamlessly," so the actions and events would move along without obvious or jarring interruptions. For many years Hollywood used certain techniques to ensure the **continuity of the story, or narrative progression**. It was accepted that for viewers to follow the story they had to be able to "read" changes in point of view, location, and time. To be able to read those changes required *continuity, based on the logic of action and story, between shots and between sequences.* Fairly strict "rules" for establishing **continuity** at both the **level of the shot** and at the **level of the sequence** evolved.

Three principles established **narrative continuity**—*the smooth forward movement of story or event*—and made the necessary changes between shots and sequences *invisible.* They were based on the **match cut**, the **establishing shot**, and the **cross-cut**. As a way of leading the viewer through the story, **transitional devices** were used that cued the viewer to changes in location or in the time frame of the action. **"Analytical editing,"** as these principles came to be called, *guided the viewer* through predictable techniques; they became the basis of the classical Hollywood cinema. The fundamental elements of classical cutting continue in use in contemporary films; others instantly signal a past era or style.

The Match Cut

The basic way to achieve smooth editing is through **matching**. *The cut is made between two shots matched by lining up either screen direction, action, graphic elements, or eyeline direction—the direction of the glance.* The first of these matches, based on **screen direction**, is the *foundation of all other match cutting.* It has been and continues to be used in all types of movies, tv shows, rock videos, and tv ads. *It establishes continuity from shot to shot and from sequence to sequence by having a character, object or the camera move in the same direction.* A rider on a horse or in a car, moving from screen right to screen left, will be picked up in the next shots, continuing from right to left. If the camera rather than the character is moving, say, panning from right to left, the pan will continue in the next shots from right to left. Matching through screen direction is consistently seen in gangster films, westerns, and contemporary adventure thrillers where that staple of the movies, the chase scene is used so often.

In the opening of JEREMIAH JOHNSON (1972), the hero of the same name (played by Robert Redford) arrives at the frontier. After he gets his mountain gear together, a series of shots shows him riding from screen right to screen left. In this case, the direction of his movement, matched from shot to shot, clearly implies his movement deeper and deeper into the wilderness.

Matching action requires that the *cut be made between two precise moments, one during the action in the first shot, the other its continuation, usually from a differing distance, in the second shot.* Cuts do not come out of the blue, just anywhere in the scene; normally they are made during a motion or a gesture, just as a character sits down or stands up, enters or exits a location. Again, in JEREMIAH JOHNSON: Johnson, starving and desperate after a bad winter in the mountains, tries to catch a fish with his bare hands. A long shot shows him as he splashes around and finally falls into the snowy creek. He starts to get up, his motion the basis of a match cut to a closer shot of him looking frustrated and then embarrassed. (The next cut, a "reverse angle," explains: an Indian is quietly watching him from the river bank.)

Matching graphic elements is another basis for a cut. *A form or pattern that relies on some element of design—a circle, square, diagonal—may be repeated from one shot to another.* In PSYCHO, Hitchcock cut from a close-up on the (circular) eye of the murdered woman to a close-up on the circle of the shower drain. Similarly, in BREATHLESS (1959), Jean-Luc Godard cuts from a close-up of an eye to a billiard ball. Subtle graphic matches occur even in less expressive, less self-conscious, more contemporary films.

The **eyeline match** (sometimes referred to as "the look of outward regard" because it always involves a character who looks "out" or off-screen) makes the cut *based on the line and direction of the glance rather than on movement.* (Refer to Figure 34.) In one sequence of CASABLANCA (1942) Rick (Humphrey Bogart), hearing the song, "As Time Goes By," angrily walks over to the piano and starts to tell Sam (Dooley Wilson) to stop playing. Sam gestures with his head, looking off to the right. Rick, following the glance, looks in the same direction and his eyes meet . . . (cut) . . . Ilse's (Ingrid Bergman), whose glance, directed left, meets his.

An illustration of the classic use of the eyeline match cut appears towards the end of that film in a sequence that shows both the bonds and the tension among Rick, Ilse and, Victor. It begins at the airport with a medium shot of the three standing on the runway, then cuts to a revving plane. On the noise of the plane, it cuts to Rick, in a close-up, as he looks to the right and then turns his head slightly from left to right. It quickly dissolves to Ilse, in a matching close-up, who is also looking right, toward the plane. She turns almost 180 degrees until her glance lines up with Rick's. A cut to a close-up of Rick, meeting her glance, shows that the two are linked. Then Rick's gaze shifts; he turns back slightly, raises his eyes, and looks off-screen, the "look of outward regard," matched in a cut to a close-up of Ilse who closes her eyes for a moment and then opens them, seeming to "return" his glance. A quick dissolve to a slightly more distant close-up of Ilse's husband, Victor Laszlo, shows that he is the point on which both Rick's and Ilse's glances converge; he looks only at Ilse. The final three-shot of the sequence shows all of them looking at one another. This exchange of glances recapitulates the whole story—the triangle, the progression of the relationships, the outcome of the story.

Figure 30. Casablanca (d. Michael Curtiz, 1942). In this still, Rick, Ilse and Victor are looking at the French soldier whose gaze meets that of Captain Reynaud. Moments later, the match cut continues the direction of the eyeline but across shots.

The Establishing Shot

One way of ensuring a match and one which used to be standard procedure in Hollywood of the 1930's, was to shoot using a **master shot** *which films an entire scene without interruption. The closer shots are later edited into the master to produce a complete sequence.* The typical sequence of shots begins with a long shot, called an **establishing shot** because *it establishes the context—the dramatic situation and the location—and orients the viewer.* Then a cut is made to a medium shot of the same subject followed by a cut to a close shot of the same subject or by shots from other angles and distances, returning to the establishing shot whenever necessary to remind the viewer of the context. This method of shooting is recognizable in the films made in the thirties, especially whenever a sudden "glamorized" close-up is inserted in the middle of a scene.

Even when this type of editing was common, directors found it useful for dramatic purposes to vary the angle and distance of the establishing shots and sometimes to wait to use the establishing shot until late in the sequence (see fig. 31). Today's filmmaking practice is much more flexible and tends to break this predictable, expected sequence of shots. Some filmmakers, especially those working in the experimental cinema or grounded in theory, deliberately set out to destroy the viewers' expectations and call into question the *place of the filmmaker and the viewer.*

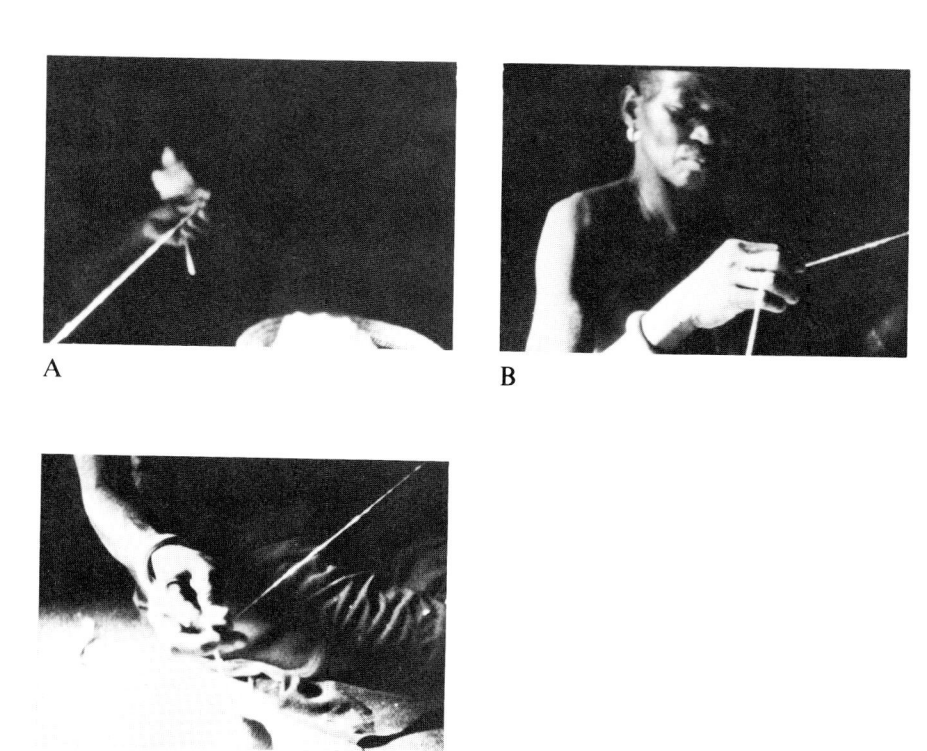

Figure 31 A, B, C. Naked Spaces: Living Is Round (d. Trinh T. Minh–ha, 1986). The filmmaker deliberately set out to break with traditional editing by resisting the use of a single establishing shot. Here the sequence seems to be a composite establishing shot but in the film the shots are actually not adjacent. In order to emphasize the *process* of spinning, shot A shows the vibrating movement of a cotton strip that extends downwards into the left corner of the frame. Shot B shows who is doing the work. Shot C completes the sequence, revealing the transformation of cotton into thread.

Cross-Cutting

Cross-cutting is another approach to establishing narrative continuity at both the level of the shot and at the level of the sequence. It continues to be used *whenever narrative threads unravel at several locations or when the director wants to produce suspense. By alternating action between at least two places,* it suggests, first, that *the action is taking place at the same time in separate locations* and, second, that *the actions will converge.* In the early days of the cinema, "cliffhangers" like THE PERILS OF PAULINE would regularly offer variations on this cross-cut sequence: shot of the heroine tied to the railroad tracks; cut to the train coming towards her; another cut to the hero riding to her rescue. The actions did, of course, converge, usually for a successful outcome. D.W. Griffith's THE LONEDALE OPERATOR (1908) cross-cuts among four locations: the telegraph operator in a train station, robbers trying to break in, another operator farther down the train line who receives the call for help, and the young engineer who races his train to the rescue.

Alfred Hitchcock relied on cross-cutting in order to generate suspense. In one sequence in NOTORIOUS, Alicia (Ingrid Bergman) and Dev (Cary Grant) are searching the wine-cellar. The shots alternate between the couple in the cellar looking for evidence of foul play, and the party above where the champagne is running low. Eventually the actions in the two locations converge as Sebastian (Claude Rains) leaves the party, goes down to the cellar to get more champagne, and sees a passionate kiss between his wife and "the other man."

Cross-cutting is essential not only to narrative fiction films but also to other forms, including documentaries and experimental films. Connie Field's THE LIFE AND TIMES OF ROSIE THE RIVETER (1978), a documentary about women working during World War II, establishes an opposition, based completely on cross-cutting, between the propaganda of that period and the contrasting real life experience of five working women. Experimental films, as well, often create visual structure and meaning through the repetition cross-cutting makes possible.

Transitions

The cut is the basic way to move from one shot to the next and while it is basically a kind of transition, it is not a device and does not "smooth" over the break in the action. **Transitional devices** *cue the viewer to changes in time, place, and action from shot to shot, scene to* *scene, location to location.* At the level of the *sequence* the same principles that required continuity required the use of **transitional devices** that would ease the viewer into the next sequence. The **fade to black**, or **fade out**, was established as a transition early on; it provides a gentle change, marking the end of a segment of action. In its day it was almost always *used to show the end of a scene* and was usually followed by a **fade in**, *the blackness lightening into an image* which *introduced a new scene in a new location.*

The **dissolve** was also commonly used in the classical cinema. This device links rather than separates the images, because two locations, scenes, or sequences are superimposed on one another and appear together on the screen for some period of time. One of the most famous dissolves in cinema must be the one that ends PSYCHO: Norman Bates' face is slowly superimposed over the face of his mummified mom to establish the "special bond" between them.

Other transitional devices—like the **iris**, *a circle that either widens into an image or narrows into a detail from the larger picture*; a **wipe**, *one image moving across the screen and "wiping off" the one already there*; a **flip frame**, *the image reversing or flipping over to reveal another*—also used to be fairly common. Certainly, a dissolve at the beginning of a flashback or connecting separate places, and the fade to show the passage of time or a change of location, were as commonplace as punctuation marks in writing. But by the 1960's, perhaps because more than a decade of constant exposure to innovative TV advertising had increased the sophistication of viewers who could now easily "read" complex image sequences, transitional devices fell out of common use in film except for calling attention to a change of location, often for humor (the wipe in BLAZING SADDLES).

The use of obvious transitional devices calls attention to the filmmaking process and usually makes the film look old-fashioned. THE MANCHURIAN CANDIDATE, a film made in 1962, felt out-dated when it was re-released in the late 1980's because shooting and editing styles had changed over the intervening twenty-five or so years and the expressive devices had become intrusive and unrealistic to the contemporary eye. The film used transitional devices, such as dissolves to introduce the characters' nightmares, wipes to show Raymond's long climb to the top of Madison Square Garden, fades to mark the end of sequences. These devices along with dramatic camera angles, break the illusion of reality.

Nowadays, except when a filmmaker deliberately employs an "old-fashioned" device to recall the past (BREATHLESS, 1959 and the Japanese film, TAMPOPO, 1987), the **straight cut**, *not necessarily matching*, is the only transition used. Whether the film sets out to experiment with form—BLUE VELVET (1986), CHOOSE ME (1984)—or is a rather standard James Bond adventure or Eddie Murphy movie, the straight cut is used to change location, action, and time. In BEVERLY HILLS COP II, for example, the opening establishes Detroit as the location. Axel Foley (Eddie Murphy), planning to investigate the murder of his pal, tells his boss that he wants to take vacation time coming to him; his boss agrees but warns him: "If you butt into this case, it'll be the longest vacation you ever heard of." The camera holds for a moment on Foley while a musical beat comes up on the sound track and then, in a straight cut, the location changes from the Detroit street at night to a low angle shot of the tall palm trees against a brilliant blue sky that is practically the "Los Angeles logo."

The Jump-Cut

The **jump-cut** is *a variation on the straight cut*. In earlier days and in an industry that operated according to the principles of smooth and invisible transitions, it was considered an error in editing. The jump-cut would only be seen when the film broke down during a screening and lost a few frames so that the movement seemed to "jump" forward. In 1959 Jean-Luc Godard changed all that in his seminal film, BREATHLESS, by deliberately choosing to use the jump-cut to change shots. *Mismatches in action and changes in angle make the film jump slightly from one shot to the next,* giving the action an irregular quality that sometimes in a humorous way, undermines the film's gangster story. Godard's intention was to call attention to the cutting itself, in order to destroy the invisible editing that had dominated filmmaking techniques until that time.

The acceptance of the film by a wide audience combined with Godard's own increasing influence and prestige as an experimental filmmaker, and the recognition by the art community and universities of alternative cinema, worked to bring the jump-cut and many other cinematic devices into the commercial cinema. The once-radical jump-cut has become a standard device used to increase tension or to produce an abrupt or shocking effect.

The Flashback and Flash Forward

The **flashback**, not strictly speaking an editing device, is *a narrative sequence that shows action that took place in the past*. It is included here because it *depends* on editing and transitional devices to set it up. Specifically, the flashback is usually *introduced by a dissolve that overlaps the two time periods*. In CASABLANCA, one scene begins with an extreme closeup of Rick's face that moves into soft focus and dissolves into another slightly soft focus shot of the Arch of Triumph in Paris. The focus becomes sharp as Rick and Ilse (in a process shot) driving in a car come into the foreground. In the flashback, Rick's memory moves forward by means of several rather slow dissolves that collapse time so that it could be spanning days, months, or hours. The flashback ends with another dissolve through the smoke from the Marseille train which moves from screen left to screen right, to Rick (picked up by the camera panning slightly, also from left to right) drinking at the table. The end of the se-

Figure 32. Casablanca. The last time Rick heard "As Time Goes By" was in those last days before the fall of France. In his memory/flashback every detail is in place.

70

quence is punctuated by the sound of the breaking glass Rick, in his pain at the memory, knocks over.

In CASABLANCA the flashback gives the reason for Rick's present circumstances; In STAND BY ME, the flashback is the whole story, framed by the dissolve at the beginning. The entire structure of CITIZEN KANE is based on interwoven flashbacks, each introduced and concluded by a dissolve. The sequence of dissolve and flashback is a standard narrative device in film.

The **flash forward** is very different. It does not follow the conventional pattern of the flashback. Whereas the interruption of the present by the past through memories and daydreams is common to our "real" experience, the interruption of the present by the *future* is not very common at all. Its appearance in movies may simply disorient viewers. For example, David Puttnam's IN DEFENSE OF THE REALM (1987) uses a straight cut to flash forward but the viewer wonders when the action is taking place. Is it real or is it a dream or a fantasy? Puttnam solves the confusion partially by using a **cut on sound**, that is, *beginning the dialogue of the next scene before the visual cut* to it, so that when the dialogue continues viewers can reorient themselves, at least in retrospect.

An unusual short science fiction film, made in France, LA JETEE ("The Jetty," 1965) uses both the flash forward and the flashback. The film, about time travel and memory, moves freely among images of the past, the present, and the future. Similarly, episodes of the TV show, "Star Trek," the movie STAR TREK IV (1987), BACK TO THE FUTURE (1985), and PEGGY SUE GOT MARRIED (1986), use flashbacks and flash forwards in a similar way, since time, in all those films, wraps around itself.

Soviet Montage

Having defined the basic editing devices, let us consider a sequence that uses editing techniques specifically to call attention to the editing process itself. Called **Soviet montage**, *it is distinguished by its use of many short takes edited together in sequences of rapidly changing images*. Sergei Eisenstein, who was most closely associated with the theory, felt that images, instead of presenting seamless "realism," should "collide" with one another, producing sequences that would jar viewers into awareness of the filmmaking process. The "Odessa Steps Sequence" from Eisenstein's film, THE BATTLESHIP POTEMKIN (1925), illustrates his "montage of conflict."

POTEMKIN: The "Odessa Steps" Sequence

The soldiers of the Czar march down the steps of the city of Odessa and move against its population to break up a minor demonstration. The director framed each shot to mark out every possible contrast: between light and dark forms, between rounded and angular shapes, between the opposing directions of the soldiers and the people, between contrasting angles and distances. The tension and conflict between the people and the Czar's soldiers are thereby presented and reinforced—all without dialogue.

The cutting between each shot is rhythmical and carefully timed to build tension. Through the editing, the action is broken down into component parts. We see the soldiers from a slight low angle, moving in formation down a long flight of steps. The sequence cuts to their rifles with bayonets fixed. Several diagonals—the downward movement of the soldiers, the steps, the rifles—are in opposition. There is a cut to a woman whose child has been injured. She lifts the child and marches back up the stairs, her movement and direction opposing and contrasting to that of the soldiers. There is a momentary hesitation in the downward movement which ends when they fire on the crowd.

The climax of the sequence comes with a cut to a mother who is shot while trying to move her baby out of harm's way. A series of close-ups, using matches as well as contrasts between graphic shapes, follows: on the face of the mother, on the baby in the carriage, on the mass of people, on the boots of the soldiers, on the wheels of the baby carriage, back to the face of the mother and then on her hands clutching her belt where she has been hit, finally to the circular wheels of the carriage. The carriage teeters on the steps, its wheels contrast with the diagonal of the step. The mother falls; all resistance by the population collapses.

At that point, the baby carriage, with no one to hold it, careens dramatically down the steps. The shots now cut from the carriage descending the steps, to the baby in the carriage, to a close-up on the carriage wheels, to the faces of horrified citizens, but always returning to the soldiers moving relentlessly down the steps, and ending with the famous close-up of the cossack raising his sword against an old woman whose broken pince-nez eye glasses and bloodied eye testify to the violence of his action.

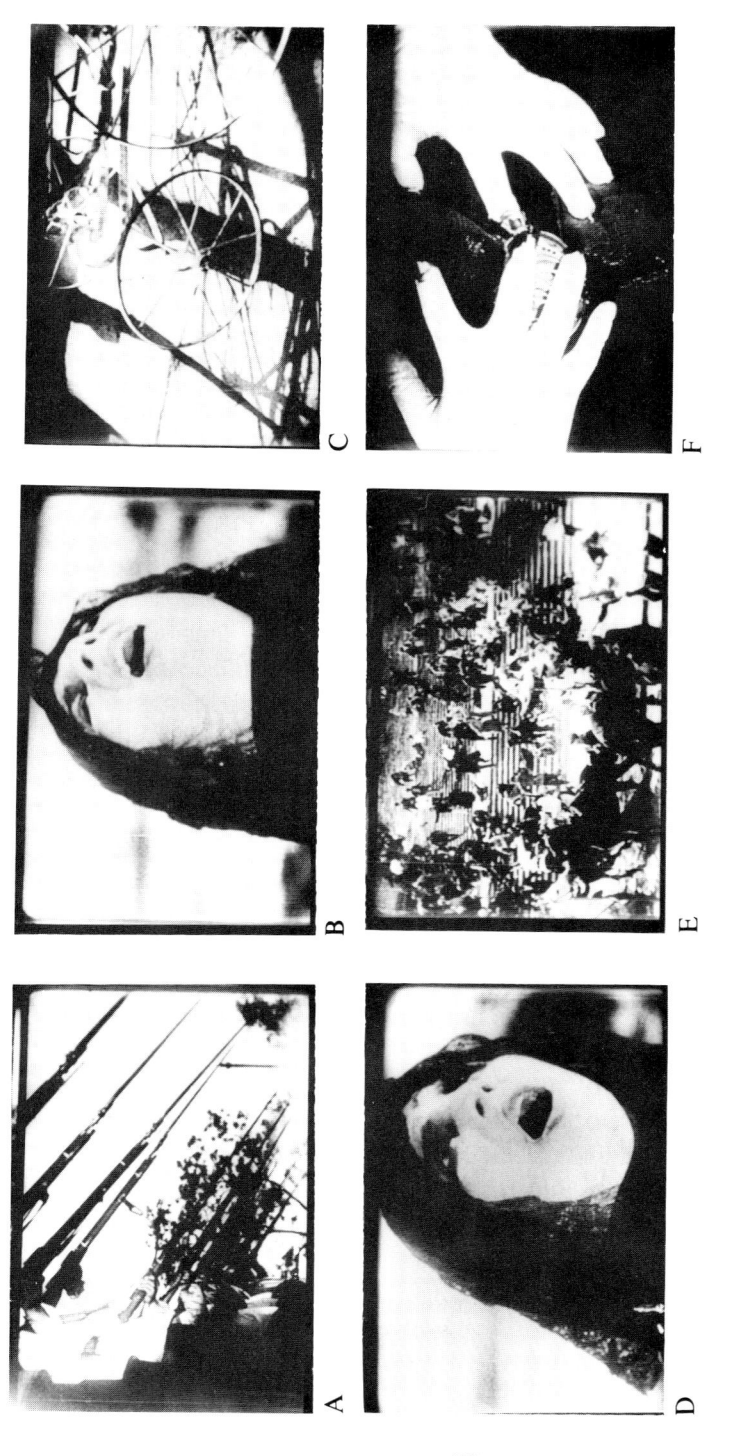

Figure 33 A–F. The Battleship Potemkin. The Odessa Steps sequence. Eisenstein creates the montage of conflict by contrasting different shapes. The circular shape of the mother's head and mouth (B and D) is repeated in the wheels of the baby carriage (C) and the belt clasp (F) and conflicts with the diagonal pattern formed by the soldiers and the angle of the perpendicular rifles (A). Shots C and E combine contrasting patterns: the round carriage wheel is on the edge of the diagonal step (C); people and Cossacks swirl against the strong horizontal lines of the steps (E). Thematically, the montage shows the opposition between the Cossack soldiers and the people.

Montage in Hollywood

"The Odessa Steps" sequence is probably the most analyzed, discussed, and familiar piece of film in the whole history of the cinema, the sequence is, in fact, so well known to students of filmmaking that some, who later became directors have "played" on it in their own films. Woody Allen may have been the first in a brief, humorous reference in BANANAS (1971). In THE UNTOUCHABLES (1987), Brian DePalma reworks the sequence giving it his own touches in a 1930's-style gangster film. These are tributes to Eisenstein by younger filmmakers who have studied the history of cinema. But the more traditional Hollywood was never very comfortable with the highly expressive approaches to film of the European filmmakers. For them, the term **montage**, (which actually comes from the French *monter*, "to mount or assemble," as in to mount a picture, or to assemble a machine), was eventually applied to a much simpler kind of editing sequence.

In Hollywood, the term "montage" meant *any sequence of rapidly edited images that suggests the passage of time or events and sketches, but does not develop, information about characters.* In INTERMEZZO (1939), the flashback of a romantic past goes by in a montage of images dissolving one into the next. Similarly, in CASABLANCA, Rick's flashback memory of his romance with Ilse is presented in a "montage" with dissolves between the shots: the couple driving in Paris, walking along the river Seine, and dancing in a nightclub. The "montage" and dissolves suggest the dreamlike quality of the memory and the timelessness of their relationship.

Currently, such commercial theatrical release films as BEVERLY HILLS COP I and II (1984 and 1987) open with a "montage" sequence, city shots cut together to give a "portrait" of Detroit. BROADCAST NEWS (1987) also uses a kind of montage to fill in the background stories of the three main characters before the beginning of the action. This kind of sequence has become standard in contemporary films.

Point of View

One of the important considerations in the study of film is how different types of shots affect the material and audience response. The primary goal of all films is to involve the viewers so that, at the least, they will keep watching. To achieve that goal, the material must be molded to create what is called "narrative suspense." The subject matter of a book or a film is presented so that it provokes curiosity: "What will happen next"? A filmmaker creates suspense by making the audience sympathize and identify with a character involved in a set of circumstances, believe in the events of the plot, and agree with the outcome. The traditional strategy to achieve all this is to connect and ally the audience with a character's *point of view.*

What is **point of view**? It is a term borrowed from literary criticism and can be thought of as *the eyes through which a reader or the viewer sees* a story or an event. In casual conversation, people commonly express notions of point of view in physical and visual terms: "What *position* are you taking on that issue?" "He's taking a certain *posture* about all that." "I've got a whole new *perspective* on it." An author might take a *stance* on or have an *attitude* about the subject or story or characters. Some common expressions parallel film terms: "What's your *take* on that?" "Here's my *angle* on that subject." "What's your *frame* of reference?" The issue actually is: Who is telling the story? Through whose eyes is the story presented? How are we asked to see the events? With whom do we empathize?

The Point of View Shot

A single **point of view (pov) shot** is technically possible as we pointed out briefly in Chapter 2. *It may be taken from any distance or angle as long as the shot logically represents what the character sees.* The *point of view shot*, also called a **subjective shot** or **first person shot** (like the "I" of a first person written narrative), shows the audience what the character is supposed to be looking at or seeing—his or her *subjective* view.

A point of view shot can be understood as a character's point of view only because of the arrangement of the shots that come before and after it. When an image of a person looking outward or off screen is followed by any other image, the viewer reads the second image as what the person in the first shot was looking at. The point of view shot may be and often is simply an **angle/reverse angle shot** which cuts together three shots. The first shot is followed by another taken from the angle opposite or nearly opposite to it. The angle/reverse angle is most often used in scenes of conversations. In simple form, it begins with a character looking off-screen, cuts to a shot of a location, person or object,and then cuts back to the face of the character looking off-screen. Each shot is framed and composed to show exactly whom each character is supposed to be looking at;

the point of view alternates between them and is matched through the "eyeline" direction.

As illustrated in Chapter 2, in certain cases the framing and composition convey the character's mood, perspective, and physical or psychological state at that moment in time. "Pov" or subjective shots are used to convey, for example, Alicia's sickness from arsenic poisoning in

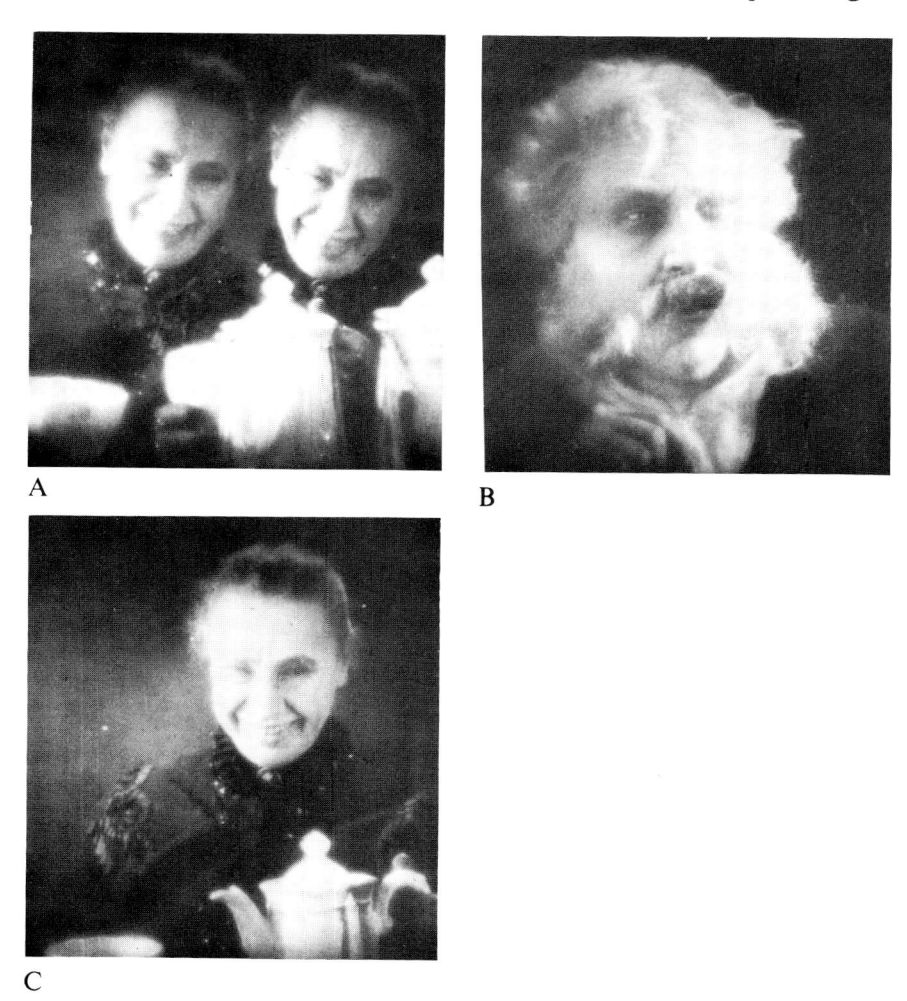

Figure 34 A, B, C. The Last Laugh. The neighbor woman offers coffee to the aging doorman. Shot A shows her "through his eyes," the double image conveying his subjective experience of waking up with a hangover. He rubs his eyes and looks again (B); this time his point of view is "normal" (C).

NOTORIOUS, the aging doorman's hangover in THE LAST LAUGH, and Scottie Ferguson's pathological fear of heights in VERTIGO (1958). What distinguishes them is that through visual alignment with the camera's position, the viewer moves from the first shot where s/he is an observer, to the second where s/he identifies with the character; at the same time, the viewer "reads" the sequence "from the outside," observing the character's emotions and actions.

The Kuleshov Experiment in Editing

This "reading" is a function of the juxtaposition of shots. and is the basis of an experiment in editing that the Soviet director, Lev Kuleshov was said to have conducted in the 1920's. As the French film historian, Jean Mitry (in his book, *Aesthetique et psychologie du cinema*) tells it, Kuleshov purposely selected a close-up shot of an actor with a vague look on his face and made 3 copies of it. He attached the first copy to a shot of a plate of soup (and here is where versions of the story vary), the second copy to a shot of a man's corpse face down on the ground, and the third to a shot of a half-nude woman posed lasciviously on a couch. *He then spliced all the shots together so that the actor's face appeared between each of the other shots.* According to observers' reports (and there is no other documentation) everyone who saw the sequence read it as a brilliant actor showing his deepest feelings first of desperate hunger, then pity, and then desire. The sequence was read in this way even though the look on the actor's face was exactly the same since it was exactly the same shot cut in each time. Whether the specific story is true or not, the psychology of perception supports the notion that viewers do interpret actors' looks and expressions from the surrounding material.

Alfred Hitchcock produced his own version of the Kuleshov experiment in REAR WINDOW (1954). In the film, L.B. Jeffries (James Stewart) is confined to a wheelchair because of a broken leg and passes the time looking out his apartment window at his neighbors. Through his telescopic camera lens he sees a musician working, newlyweds moving into their apartment, a lonely spinster drinking, a dancer practicing, a couple bickering. Hitchcock cuts back and forth from shots of each person's activities to Jeff's face. As in the original experiment, the shot of Jeff's face is the same one repeated; Hitchcock intended the audience to "read" the "range" of Jeff's emotions: pity, approval, lust, amusement, curiosity. His look does seem to change, depending on what he is looking

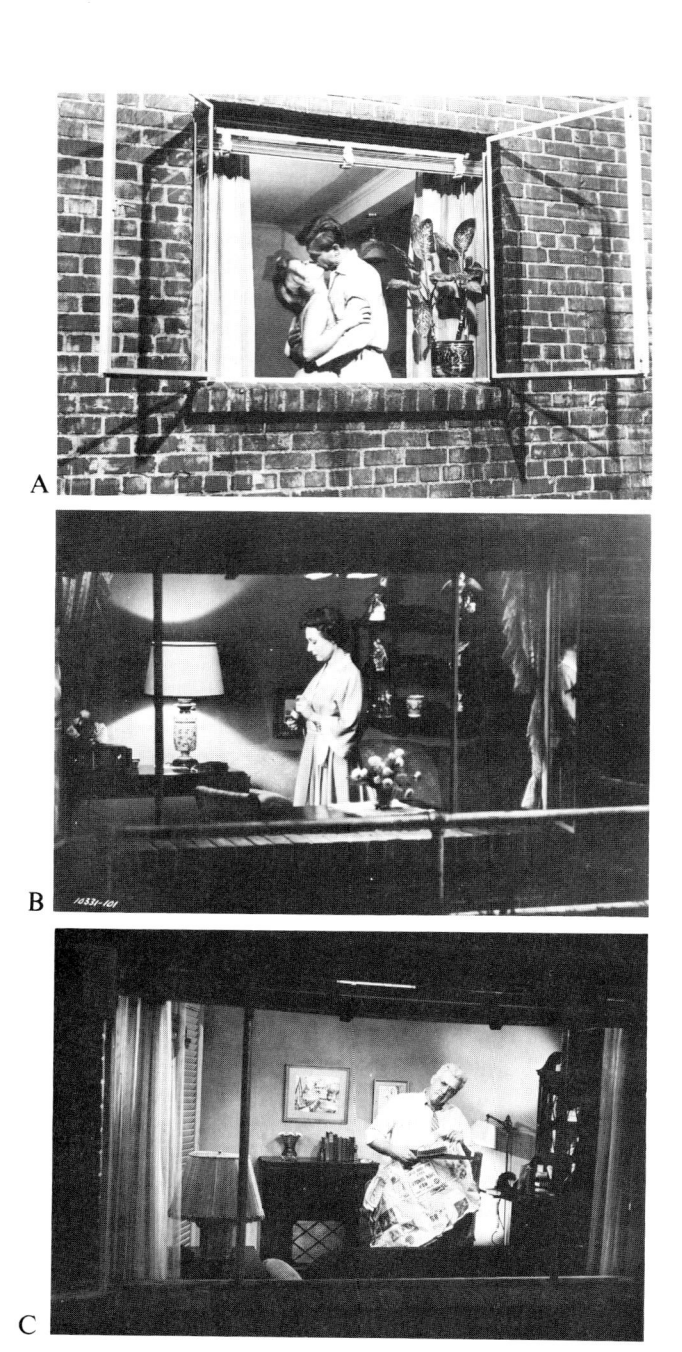

Figure 35 A, B, C. Rear Window (d. Alfred Hitchcock, 1957). Hitchcock's version of the "Kuleshov experiment." The same shot of James Stewart's face (fig. 35D), looking through his telephoto lens, is intercut between shots of activities in the apartments across the courtyard.

Figure 35 D. Rear Window. The character, Jeff, seems to respond differently to each of the scenes.

at. Why does this occur? It seems to be a function of the viewer's need to make sense and meaning out of the separate shots.

Point of View and the Narrator

In both written fiction and in film, point of view relates to the narrator, the teller of the story. In writing, the narrator's voice and perspective are conveyed, of course, through *words*. There are several possible narrative "voices" in written fiction but, although individual films have tried to achieve the broad range open to written fiction, we need to concern ourselves here only with two of the narrative voices because fiction films use them most commonly.

One kind of narrator is deeply involved in the events, telling the story from the first person, "I." The narrator of Herman Melville's *Moby Dick* begins his story by introducing himself: "Call me Ishmael." Another type is detached from the events, telling the story as an objective third person, "he" or "they": "Stately, plump Buck Mulligan came from the stairhead, bearing a bowl of lather on which a mirror and a razor lay crossed," says the narrator of James Joyce's *Ulysses*.

Films are also a story-telling medium and, in a way similar to literature (if somewhat more limited), they may either situate the narrator *within* the story, or present him/her as an outside observer. In the first case, the narrator tells the story from his personal perspective, having lived through the events. The detective story, MURDER, MY SWEET (made in 1944 from a Raymond Chandler novel), is an example. Private investigator Philip Marlowe (Richard Powell) tells the police, who are holding him for murder, about the circumstances leading to his arrest. Just as in the many other films that use a narrator to "frame" the story, we hear Marlowe's voice and then see, in a flashback, the past events in which Marlowe has been involved. Films that tell stories in the first person almost always use the story-teller's narrating voice over a flashback. Once the flashback begins, the presentation of events is usually objective and unfolds in the "present tense"; while the framing narration (and occasional returns to the "real" present) lets the viewer know that those events took place in the past (see fig. 36).

LADY IN THE LAKE (1946), taken from another Raymond Chandler detective novel, experimented with the convention of the first-person narrator. In this film, the director, Robert Montgomery, set out to reproduce Chandler's characteristic hard-boiled, first-person voice by making the entire film from subjective camera angles only. The camera

Figure 36. Murder, My Sweet (d. Edward Dmytryk, 1944). Philip Marlowe in the flashback. "Film noir" lighting shows strong black and white areas using "motivated" light sources so that pools of light and shadows form on the walls. The key is the "key" point of interest in center frame.

"was" Marlowe and only "saw" what Marlowe could see so except for a glimpse in a mirror, the audience never saw Marlowe himself and it was difficult to identify with the hero. What's worse, a camera is not very good at such regular, hard-boiled detective activities as smoking, kissing, and fighting. It does a better job of showing than participating. The experiment turned out to be clunky and awkward. The first-person camera has been used mainly to underline, briefly, a character's point of view; as the basis of an entire film, it presents serious problems. It is most interesting as a study of the use of the point of view shot.

Films that tell stories from the third person, the "objective" point of view, are much more common. The camera easily fills the place of an outside narrator because it *normally* records so-called "objective reality." Of course, even in these "objective" narratives, the camera will often present the point of view of one of the characters in a point of view shot, or a subjective shot to show a more complex visual image that expresses the character's feelings about his/her situation or sometimes in a simple reverse angle shot to show a conversation.

The camera creates the character's point of view by taking his or her place. A shot looks neutral or menacing depending on who is supposed to be doing the looking. For example, by itself, the high angle shot is only one out of many possible shots. But if it suggests or is identified as that of a killer perched at the top of the stairs looking down at a victim or of an Indian brave ready to attack, it takes on menace and threat. The point of view may be linked to a character through a **pov** shot, or it may be "objective," outside any one character, but even when the camera remains "objective" and does not take a specific character's specific point of view, the camera always creates a point of view.

Conclusion

Editing, along with the pre-production procedures of scripting and storyboarding, converts hundreds of individual shots into a connected, coherent, understandable, and dramatic presentation of information or story. The process of editing arranges sequences that orient and involve the viewer in an imaginary space and that develop symbols and themes. The power of editing is illustrated by its creation of point of view which is one of the most important story-telling strategies for film because it enables us to identify with a character and experience events from his/her position. It does this by establishing point of view. If we can say that the shot provides the cinema with its visual dimension by allowing the camera to imitate the human eye—looking at objects and people from close up, far away, above or below; and if movement provides the physical dimension by allowing it to imitate the human body—moving freely through locations; then editing provides the intellectual dimension because it constructs meaning and tells a story. Editing *is* the art of the movies.

CHAPTER 5
Sound

Most people think of film as a completely visual medium and yet when they are asked to talk about a movie they often repeat snatches of dialogue or tell the story rather than describing images. Obviously film is *primarily* a visual medium, but **sound** is an almost equal part of all movies. Sometimes the *music* heard in a film will trigger a memory of the visual images: probably most people have had the experience of recognizing a tune even when they don't know its name. But if they've seen the movie, hearing Strauss' *Thus Spake Zarathustra* will doubtless make them think of 2001: A SPACE ODYSSEY. Similarly, the music from STAR WARS, heard even in an elevator, makes many people think of the characters and scenes in that movie.

Music, while probably most memorable, is not the only important sound that contributes to emotion and meaning. A line of dialogue, "Play it, Sam. Play 'As Time Goes By'," will immediately make those who saw the film smile and remember CASABLANCA (1942) and perhaps the melody as well.

A Historical Note

Sound has been part of movies for fifty out of the eighty years of film history so we tend to take it for granted; yet its contribution, although not always obvious, is much more complex than it might seem. To start with, let us consider sound in its historical context. The fact that originally films were silent, seems at first glance to reinforce the idea that the medium is essentially visual and does not really need sound. But even the earliest silent films had musicians and sometimes narrators to accompany them. And almost from the beginning, attempts were made to find a way to attach sound to the picture. Only two years after the invention of movies, Thomas A. Edison was experimenting with ways of synchronizing sound and image. Others, in France as well as in the United States, had some moderate success with sound in short films as early as 1909.

Despite popular interest, "sound films" could not be widely distributed at that time because the technology was not yet perfected and problems of synchronization and amplification were far from resolved. In fact, technological limitations (and the resulting skepticism of some producers) prevented sound film from getting past the novelty stage until the 1920's.

The "silent" film, then, was never really silent. Just about every movie house had musical accompanists; even the most humble had at least a piano and usually a violinist as well. The musical accompaniment was a natural outcome of showing the movies to working class people in music halls and vaudeville theatres. As the movies became more popular, exhibitors designed and built special movie theatres. Some producers, recognizing the potential appeal of the movies to a larger, middle-class audience, wanted to make the new medium more respectable and began to improve the quality of the films and the screenings. As early as 1908 musical scores were being composed for films and exhibitors were acquiring grander theatres equipped with full orchestras and magnificent organs to play them.

Music was not the only type of sound provided in those early film screenings. Some theatres hired sound effects specialists who would sit in the orchestra pit or behind the screen and create sounds—thundering hooves, a gunshot, rain drops—at appropriate moments in the story. Special sound effects machines—for example, the Noiseograph and the Excelsior Sound Effect Cabinet—were developed. Sometimes a Master of Ceremonies acted as a live commentator who explained the film, told the story, spoke dialogue for one of the characters, or gave details about the film's production. Companies of "actors" sprang up which specialized in presenting dialogue from behind the screen. Sound was clearly a concern long before technology made *sound-on-film* possible.

What, then, made the "coming of sound" in 1927 so significant? Before the development of an efficient system for combining sound and image, every time sound was used, whether music, effects, or a commentator, it was really a *live performance* and therefore both expensive and unpredictable. And technical minds were frustrated by their inability to reproduce the voices of the actors and the background sounds of life to go along with the visual illusion of reality that they were able to create.

***

To be able to record and play back realistic sound, the visual track and the sound track must be perfectly **synchronized**. That means *the sound recording equipment has to record material at exactly the same*

Figure 37. Saving the Proof. An enlarged photograph of three frames shows the sprocket holes on the left and the optical sound track on the right of the 16mm film. Sounds are converted into the optical patterns printed on the film and read by the projector's exciter lamp which converts them back to sound. Sound quality may be better recorded on magnetic tape, but optical sound is easier to use and cheaper to distribute.

speed as the camera: the camera picks up the image at precisely the same time as the microphone picks up the sound. Then the two tracks have to be played back at precisely the same speed. The slightest discrepancy in timing will put the picture "out of sync" so that lips might visibly mouth one word while the sound track "speaks" the next; a door might close silently followed a second later by the slam; a gangster might pull the trigger of a gun followed by the sound of the shot a moment later.

The film SINGIN' IN THE RAIN (1952) provides a humorous but instructive illustration of the difficulties studios faced during their conversion to sound. The story is set in 1929, on the eve of the "sound era," at a Hollywood studio producing its first sound picture. Every possible problem arises: the heroine's voice is all wrong for her part; once dialogue is added, the actors' silent-film style delivery and gestures look too theatrical; the primitive microphone picks up and magnifies some sounds—the rustle of costumes, the rattle of jewelry, the clatter of the actors's footsteps—but misses important dialogue. To make matters worse, the sound track slowly goes "out of sync" until the dashing hero seems to be speaking the heroine's lines in a shrill, squeaky voice while she seems to speak in his deep voice. SINGIN' IN THE RAIN chronicles, in a musical comedy, many of the nightmares that really did plague the early sound productions. But since the problems were actually overcome rather quickly, for us the movie remains an amusing and accurate reminder of the way sound works in film.

In the early days of sound recording, if any synchronized sound was to be used, *all* sound—music, sound effects, non-synchronous dialogue—had to be recorded on the set at the same time. But by the early 1930's directors had learned to *mix* "sync" sound with sound recorded elsewhere and add it during the post-production stage. Directors, freed from the limitations of on-the-spot recording and recognizing the potential of the new sound techniques, began to use them to achieve esthetic goals. For example, in 1929, in his first sound film, BLACKMAIL (1929), Alfred Hitchcock gradually decreased the volume during a conversation about a murder. The guilty heroine's terror grows visibly as she (and the audience) hear nearly nothing of the neighbor's conversation except for the single word, "knife," the murder weapon. Here, Hitchcock manipulated sound to emphasize psychological effects to increase the drama.

Josef von Sternberg's THE BLUE ANGEL, made in Germany in 1931, offers another example of the interesting use of sound. As the film begins, a maid is busily setting up a breakfast table. She does not speak while she is working, but we hear the sounds of her activity—doors closing, clink of coffee pot on the table—all very realistic. She calls her employer to breakfast and, as Herr Rath arrives, the sounds die away to complete silence as he pulls out his chair, pours his coffee and begins his breakfast. The sound returns as he whistles over his shoulder. Hearing no response, he gets up and, whistling again, goes over to a bird cage where he finds his bird dead. The silence has foreshadowed the canary's death which foreshadows the story's tragic ending. This film made in the early sound period, Von Sternberg has already shifted his emphasis from a purely realistic use of sound to a symbolic one.

A few years later, in THE 39 STEPS (1935), Hitchcock worked out a brilliant "sound cut." The landlady finds a dead woman's body in the hero, Richard Hannay's apartment. We see her open her mouth to scream but instead of hearing the scream, we hear the sound of a screeching train whistle. The sound cut is immediately followed by a visual cut to the train which, it turns out, is carrying the fleeing Hannay. The cut on the scream-whistle called attention to the innovative possibilities of sound and at the same time moved the story forward in a dramatic way.

Figure 38. The Blue Angel. The only sound in this part of the sequence is Herr Rath's unanswered whistle. The absence of other sounds, music, or dialogue magnifies the silence and prepares for the discovery of the canary's death.

It is impossible to discuss innovative uses of sound practice without mentioning Orson Welles. Welles came to Hollywood from a very successful radio show called The Mercury Theatre. In 1939, he stunned the whole radio-listening country with his show, "The War of the Worlds," in which he transmitted a "news report" on an invasion from Mars. Despite several interruptions reminding listeners that they were hearing a story, Welles' clever use of the news reporter style and sound effects were so realistic that people panicked. That broadcast ended Welles' radio career but opened the door to Hollywood.

Naturally Welles brought to Hollywood extensive experience with the way radio used sound, for example as a transitional device similar to the editing devices normally used to create visual continuity. In CITIZEN KANE, the young Charles Kane "grows up" in the course of only two images *connected through sound*. In the first, he is a young boy receiving a Christmas gift from his guardian, Thatcher, who begins a greeting, "A Merry Christmas. . . ." In the next shot Thatcher finishes the wish, ". . . and a Happy New Year," to Kane, now a young man. The visual cut is made continuous through the sound transition.

Another device, **overlapping dialogue**, which is *dialogue spoken by several characters at the same time,* was also very innovative for its time. At the beginning of TOUCH OF EVIL (1958), a time bomb blows up a car; a curious crowd immediately gathers. The hero (Charlton Heston) dashes onto the scene along with the police and newspapermen. Cars arrive, sirens wail, and *everybody talks at once*, interrupting one another in their excitement. Despite the overlapping of both voices and sound effects, the viewer hears everything important to the story through the sound engineer's careful control of the volume as each person speaks. Nothing is actually lost; the viewer is not confused; yet a realistic atmosphere is established.

Kinds of Sound

In just the few examples above, we have mentioned several different kinds of sound: music, conversation and dialogue, activity noises. The range of sound possibilities is nearly infinite. So are the ways in which sounds may be integrated with one another. For our discussion, two categories of sound—**synchronous sound**, that is, *sound occurring at the same time as the image that produces it*, and **non-synchronous sound**, that is, *sound occurring separately from the image,*—can be established. These two categories can be divided further into *music, dialogue, narration,* and *sound effects.*

Synchronous and Non-Synchronous Sound

As we have already pointed out, the development of a system that could produce reliable *synchronous* sound made the "talkie" possible. But it would be a mistake to assume that all film sound was synchronous after 1927, when Al Jolson delivered his historic line in THE JAZZ SINGER: "You ain't heard nothin' yet." Although Hollywood suddenly began to produce a great many plays because dialogue and delivery could now be accurately recorded and shown, after a short time directors realized that they did not have to limit themselves to works that relied on synchronous sound; almost any sound that they used synchronously could also be used non-synchronously.

Sound on is sound whose *source is visible in the images on the screen*, like a record player or radio playing the music we hear. **Sound off** is sound whose *source is not in the images on the screen*. The two are usually used together to create an auditory "world" that enhances, expands, or expounds upon the visual images. Crucial as "sound on" is to the viewer's sense of reality, "sound off" is used far more often. Many productions—documentaries, educational films, news segments, short fiction films, animation, experimental works, MTV, advertisements, and student films—have been made with *no* synchronous sound at all. Contrary to popular opinion very few films are made with *only* synchronous sound.

Let us look here at the ways synchronous and non-synchronous sound are used.

Music

Except for dialogue, *music is the sound most used in movies*. We will deal with it first because it supports all types of film, features, documentaries, experimental works, and animation. After all, it was the original accompaniment and already an accepted and expected element before sound *on* film even became possible. Although there are film forms entirely dependent on music, such as musical comedies, concert performance films, biographies of musicians, and "rock docs," as they are called, these will not concern us here because the music in those films is the *subject* of the film and contributes differently to meaning and interpretation.

Music that provides interpretation is the non-synchronous, "background music," used in fiction films to underline an image or to carry a mood and is as important to the production of meaning as dialogue or narration. In certain cases, the music actually functions *like* narration, describing the action in a scene and giving information about it. At other times the music "translates" emotions, provokes responses, and sets up psychological associations. Is the action suspenseful? Frightening? Terrifying? Romantic? Humorous? Poignant? Nostalgic? Sad? Audiences can be cued to a whole range of emotional responses by the music and that has been one reason why movie ads could confidently promise—and deliver—thrills, chills, laughter, and tears.

Composers and musicians know that very slow, fast, high, low or staccato sounds generate tension, whereas melodic and harmonic music have the opposite effect and they have regularly manipulated certain frequencies of sound and its extremes in order to affect audiences whether they were writing for films, television show, radio shows, or drama. Consider the image of a sleeper. The person's expression is calm, the breathing even. When soft music is played with the image, it produces a perfect picture of tranquility. A violin added suggests romantic, "sweet" dreams. A subdued saxophone might suggest sadness instead. But bring in the bass and a slow, measured drum beat and tension increases. Continue to build on the beat, change the melodic violin to a shrill pitch, and the mood changes into a nightmare or the threat of approaching evil. If an image-sound pattern were actually analysed this way, the results would have to parallel those of the Kuleshov experiment in cutting: the image would remain the same and this time because of the change in the music, the viewer's interpretation of and response to the image would change.

Background Music

Background music is applied to fiction films so that it *refers to the film,* anchoring the image to meaning and creating emotional associations. Another way to put it is that image and music relate to one another by what one film critic, Claudia Gorbman has called "**mutual implication**," by which she means that *images give meaning to music just as music gives meaning to images.* The image of the sleeper mentioned above is a good example of this reciprocal relationship. Another is the very direct, music-image interaction of rock videos. There too the relationship between music and image is a mutual one because the music and the images comment on, interpret, and affect one another.

But to call the relationship a "mutual" one should not suggest that the music and image track are equal. The music in a film (unless it is a concert film), always takes second place to the image because it must first meet the *dramatic needs* of the story and also *fit with sound effects and dialogue.* A film's musical score, when *mixed* with the other sound tracks—dialogue, background sound, sound effects (many sound effects are actually *designed* to coincide with a musical key)—becomes integrated with them and with the image. Music is only one element in the elaborate sound construction created around the images during the *post-production* phase.

Certain critics have taken a theoretical position against "parallel composition" in which the music "repeats" the images—a passionate embrace is seen while romantic music is heard; they wrote in favor of **counterpoint**, that is, music and sounds *contrast* with the image. However, most music written for or applied to visual forms underlines and supports the image. First in the silent cinema and later in the sound film, movie music was used to illustrate the image or create a mood, and that relationship continues pretty much unchanged in today's films.

Hundreds of years before film was even conceived of, musicians were composing music that described subject matter. In the fourteenth century composers used "word-painting" to suggest a "picture" of what the song was about. Over the years, and using different styles, composers wrote music that would tell stories in melodies. By the nineteenth century, "word-painting" had evolved into the **"leitmotif,"** which translates from German as *a musical theme that represents a person, idea or quality*. The composers associated with the development of the *"leitmotif"* are Richard Wagner in opera, and Peter Tschaikovsky in the "tone poems," especially "Peter and the Wolf." Composers assigned a musical phrase or theme to each character and situation and whenever either appeared, the theme or a variation on it was played, eventually weaving together throughout the piece.

Film music followed in the tradition of classical music. In the silent period the accompanist would select and then play musical phrases that he felt would identify characters and set the right mood. When music began to be written specifically for film, composers continued this sort of composition; *at the appearance of a character or situation a theme was played and slightly varied* and became a **motif** associated with the character or situation. To a large extent themes continue to be used in this way today.

In M (1931), the murderer (played by Peter Lorre) whistles a fragment of the "Hall of the Mountain King" from Edvard Grieg's *Peer Gynt Suite*. For a time the audience does not see the murderer (except for his shadow or back) but comes to connect the repeated tune with him. The connection is echoed within the film when a blind street seller, especially sensitive to sounds because of his disability, hears the whistled tune, makes the connection, and points out the killer.

In the films of John Ford a very different tone and mood are created. Ford used musical motifs especially in his westerns where traditional American hymns sung by the characters and playing as themes on the soundtrack, underscore the strength of the "community." For example, the hymn, "Shall we Gather By the River," is used in several films at burials to convey communal strength and unity in the face of death. Musical motifs also link couples romantically and establish individual or group identities. In Ford's classic, STAGECOACH (1939), Ringo (John Wayne) and Dallas (Claire Trevor) are linked to a melody, repeated in the story and finally sung by an Apache woman that associates the couple with the West. Whenever the Cavalry appears, the ballad, "I Dream of Jeannie with the Light Brown Hair," about a girl left behind in the East, is heard. Images of the stagecoach are accompanied by an upbeat, orchestrated version of "Bury Me Not On the Lone Prairie," that emphasizes both the lurking threat of death in the coach's path and the courage to continue of the stage and its passengers. Of course, the Indians are associated with a drum beat rhythm that later became such an obvious cliche of the Hollywood Western that it indicated their ominous presence even when they were not on screen.

In a very different type of western made many years later, LITTLE BIG MAN (1970), (which will be examined in detail in Chapter 7), one recurrent musical motif is the fife and drum tune of the United States Cavalry. After each of the several massacres of women and children, the fife and drum are heard. The tune, associated with the Civil War and with a more gallant cavalry of earlier western films, becomes painfully ironic, underscoring the cruelty and genocide perpetrated by General George Armstrong Custer's military troops as they move against the Indians.

Among Europeans, the Italian director Federico Fellini and his longtime musical collaborator, Nino Rota, worked together from the early days of the director's career (LA STRADA, 1954) through almost all of his films, including LA DOLCE VITA (1960) and 8 1/2 (1963). Rota's music informs the viewer's "reading" of the characters blends motif with character and incident.

In LA STRADA, Gelsomina the clown (the heroine played by Giulietta Massina), learns to play the trumpet for her brutish employer Zampano's (Anthony Quinn) circus. She learns a simple, melancholy, haunting tune, from a much kinder tightrope artist (Richard Basehart), Zampano's principle antagonist, and plays it over and over. At the end, Zampano returns to the town where he deserted Gelsomina and hears the melody sung by a local woman. When he first heard the tune he dismissed it and Gelsomina; this time he is tormented by it and by the memory of Gelsomina. Because of the song, in fact through it, Zampano comes to realize that he had not valued the beauty Gelsomina brought to his life and he is made more human by suffering the painful loss.

The Italian folk tunes that inspired Rota in the early Fellini films, and the simple American hymns and folksongs used extensively by John Ford, stand in contrast to the lush, rich, romantic, European-style compositions of Miklos Rozsa, Bernard Herrmann, and Max Steiner, who worked during the 1940's and 1950's. Writing for Hitchcock, Welles, and the directors of the thrillers known as the "film noir," these composers wrote music that typically, "clues" the audience to the emotional feeling the scene is supposed to create: suspense, romance, hope, to name a few.

For PSYCHO, Bernard Herrmann wrote background music that, together with symbolic elements, narrative structure, and sound effects,

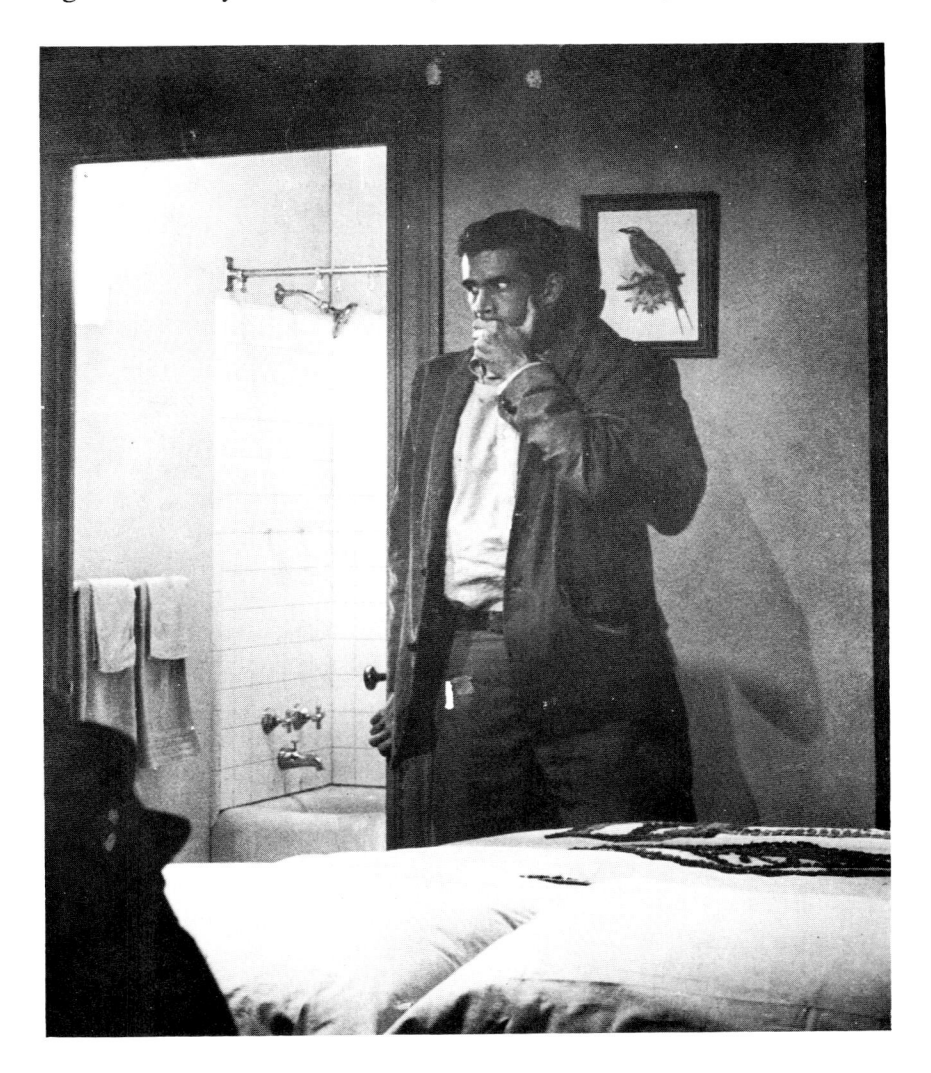

Figure 39. Psycho (d. Alfred Hitchcock, 1960). Norman is horrified by what his "mom" has done. The film builds the bird motif through sound and visuals. On the audio track, bird sounds are heard. The picture of the bird on the wall is echoed in Norman's posture, his claw-like hand over his mouth, the shape of his jacket, and wing-like shadow of his arm on the wall.

sets up a complex association between Norman Bates and birds. It runs through the whole film: the name of the murdered woman is Marion *Crane*; she chats with Norman one night in a room decorated with stuffed birds; when she begins to eat the snack he has prepared for her, he tells her she eats like a bird. Visually, there are many subtle references. The association is extended on the sound-track where the music, ambient sound, silence, dialogue, and sound effects work together not only to continue the "birds" theme, but also to generate suspense (see fig. 39). When Norman invites Marion into his parlor for a bite to eat, only realistic noises, no exterior ambient sounds are heard during their chat. But when Marion casually suggests that he consider putting his invalid mother "someplace," he is horrified and upset. His voice rises as he says: "You mean an institution? A *madhouse?*" At that exact moment, along with a change in camera angle, very low-pitched music with a repeating beat begins and continues quietly until Marion leaves to return to her room, when a higher-pitched violin, resembling the sound of screeching birds, begins over the low tones. The music stops entirely and, once again, only natural sounds are heard during the next two transitional scenes. Then comes the shower scene.

At first only the natural sounds of a person showering are heard: the shower curtain being pulled, the water running and falling. Suddenly the shower curtain is pulled back and at the same moment, a high-pitched, bird-like shriek (violin) merges with Marion's scream. The violin shrieks and human screams continue while Marion is stabbed until the killer runs off and she is dead. The alternation of low-pitched music, high-pitched sounds, and silence create and sustain suspense. Later, in the scene of the murder of Detective Arbogast, the high-pitched, bird-like shrieks used over the shower sequence are repeated but raised to an even more disturbing level. The bird-like sounds, added to the bird's eye shot and a hawk-like, downward-swooping motion of the kill, all sustain the "bird motif."

In these two sequences (and elsewhere in the film), the music is one important thread in the intricate fabric of sounds. In PSYCHO generally, sound actually more important to the production of anxiety and suspense than are the images. It is nearly impossible not to be frightened by the two murders. But if the sound is turned off (through the powerful VCR), the viewer can watch the sequence quite "calmly," proving that it is not primarily the images but rather the sound that creates the suspense and fear.

Sometimes music that sustains the mood does not have to be written specifically for the film. Well-known popular songs are also used to sup-

Figure 40. Psycho. In the famous shower sequence, Marion screams, the sound merging with high-pitched, bird-like shrieking on the sound track.

port image, theme, and story. Many *"period pieces,"* **films set in a specific historical moment,** rely on songs of the time to give authenticity to the film. George Lucas made AMERICAN GRAFFITI in 1972 but set it in 1962. Wanting to "recreate" the California of his home town, Modesto, in the late 1950's and early '60's, he found the right cars, clothes, hairstyles, and slang of the period. But the single element that gives the true "feel" of the era is the Rock 'n' Roll music on the soundtrack. Songs were used as a believable background to the cruising, dating, fighting, and dancing, necessary to the portrayal of the characters—but also the words to the songs offer a a subtle running commentary on their lives.

In two autobiographical films, Woody Allen's RADIO DAYS (1986) and Neil Simon's BRIGHTON BEACH MEMOIRS (1987), the music of the thirties supports and defines the stories of growing up during the Depression. Other films set in the more recent past use exactly appropriate songs. In some cases they recreate a specific year: for DESERT BLOOM (1986) it is 1950, for THE RIGHT STUFF (1983) it is 1956; BACK TO THE FUTURE (1985) "returns" to 1955. And each story depends on the popular songs of the time to orient the viewer.

Music is basic to the film medium. While it may be the basis of an entire film and capture attitudes and tastes or document entertainment in performance films, *its major importance lies in its capacity to produce meaning.* As we have seen, music is used in fiction features as background and support to the image and is as important to meaning in film as dialogue or sound effects. Through "mutual implication" music can be used to anchor the significance of the image, to intensify its emotional qualities, to comment ironically on it, and to foreshadow events in the story.

Dialogue

Most of us take dialogue in films as much for granted as we do music and, of course, it was a necessary part even of silent movies, where *intertitles* written on the screen presented the conversations and dramatic lines of the characters to continue the story. **Dialogue** consists of *lines of speech spoken in conversation between two or among more characters.* Every type of film depends on *speech,* whether a fiction film which needs *words to tell the story* or a documentary which needs *words to convey information or present a position* on a subject. Only those experimental films concerned completely with the visuals use no dialogue. Words may be on-screen or heard off-screen as background conversation; they may be the highly-charged language of drama, or the amusing remarks of comedy; but movies depend on them. The movies were called "talkies" when sound first arrived.

Not all dialogue occurs **on camera**, *synchronized with the image.* In fact, a great deal is actually spoken **off camera**. *The words may be spoken to another character while the listener appears on the screen,* perhaps the most common example of off-camera dialogue. This is the **shot-reverse angle shot**, where, instead of cutting from one speaker to the next, the film will very often cut to a *reaction* shot that shows *the listener responding to the speaker.* The effect of the words is visible, communicated by a combination of the listener's expression and the words off-camera.

Dialogue may operate as a transitional device, beginning on-camera and continuing for a short time after the new shot is on-screen, or vice versa, beginning off-screen and continuing as dialogue in the next shot. This use of dialogue can make a cut invisible and is common although it often goes unnoticed. A sound bridge will usually involve only a few words, but the dialogue may go on at length as the camera calls attention to a visual sign of significant information—the speaker's hands, for example, or an object referred to in the dialogue. Sound cuts or sound transitions are rapidly becoming standard form in feature films, noticeable in everything from a James Bond movie, THE LIVING DAYLIGHTS (1987) to a fairytale like THE PRINCESS BRIDE (1987).

    The three types of sound—**synchronous dialogue, on-camera non-synchronous dialogue, and off-camera dialogue**—can work together in important ways. Robert Altman, known for his manipulation of sound, has developed a style that includes overlapping dialogue. He has been accused by producers and critics of making all his actors talk at the same time, thereby making it impossible to understand what is going on in the

Figure 41. McCabe And Mrs. Miller (d. Robert Altman, 1971).
Warren Beatty and Julie Christie in the title roles seen in the bar.
The sound in the film is characterized by over-lapping and indistinct background conversations.

picture. In MCCABE AND MRS. MILLER (1971), the overlay of dialogue and sound effects—speakers on-camera and off-camera, ambient noise, and conversation that appears to be on-camera, yet never clearly associated with a specific source—is so dense that it is often difficult to understand McCabe's words the delivery of which Warren Beatty, as McCabe, was directed to "mumble." The interwoven dialogue created in this way, although frustrating to the viewer, also creates a high degree of realism, makes it more like "life," since speech is not always directed to a privileged listener. Altman seems to prevent the viewer from hearing everything clearly, but that lack changes the relationship to the film requiring the viewer to search the image for clues to the dialogue and the narrative.

On another level, the theme of the film is communication and the lack of it. The story is finally about the relationship between an inarticulate man and a woman who, unavailable emotionally, prefers to retreat into drug-induced dreams; their communication is so minimal that they are unable either to negotiate with or struggle against a "corporate" takeover.

Narration

Narration, as it applies to issues of sound, *refers to the telling of a story by a voice heard on the sound track.* By common convention, narration is almost always *voice-over narration* and is used in both fiction and documentary film. In fiction, the narrator relates events that s/he has lived through and which are then seen in the images on the screen. In documentaries, especially those made between 1930 and 1950, an unseen but very authoritative narrator presents informational material about the subject of the film. The novel, of course, commonly uses both first and third person narration; the voice-over as a conventional device carried on this strategy in radio plays and, eventually, it became commonplace in film.

In fiction films, the narrator is usually seen only briefly *as a narrator* before he or she becomes a participating character in the story he or she is relating. Examples occur in CITIZEN KANE, where several characters are interviewed and begin to tell the story of their experience with Charles Foster Kane. As they speak, a slow dissolve, keeping them on the screen for a short time, shifts the scene to past events in which they appear as their younger selves. In one case, that of Kane's guardian, Mr. Thatcher, the "narrator" is actually only his diary, read by the interviewer; the dissolve begins on handwritten pages rather than on the character himself. Voice-over narration frames each of the stories, another dissolve at the end of the segment returning the action to the "present."

In the thriller and detective films of the 1930's and '40's, the voice-over introduced a character, usually the protagonist, who was deeply involved in complicated events and who told the story in the first person—"I." MURDER, MY SWEET (1946), DOUBLE INDEMNITY (1945), THE POSTMAN ALWAYS RINGS TWICE (1945), OUT OF THE PAST (1947), SUNSET BOULEVARD (1950), among many others, used this conventional device of voice-over combined with the dissolve to transport the action into the past.

While voice-over narration was most used during the post-war years, it continues to be used relatively often today. The characters may participate within the story, as in STAND BY ME, LITTLE BIG MAN, and SHE'S GOTTA HAVE IT (1986), or they may remain unseen, disembodied as in RADIO DAYS (1986), DESERT BLOOM (1986), HOPE AND GLORY (1987). Arthur Penn's LITTLE BIG MAN (1970) begins with a very old "Indian fighter" (Dustin Hoffman) insisting in an interview that he survived Custer's Last Stand. In response to the interviewer's skepticism—because in fact there were no "white survivors"—he begins to narrate the story of his life. A long flashback opens and he is not seen again in the "present," as an old man, until the end of the film. He "returns" as a voice on the sound track, intervening at significant moments to comment in hindsight on the youthful errors of his life. In CITIZEN KANE narrators are "literary," framing each segment, presenting each individual narrative, and commenting on the information but, in the final analysis, leaving the details ambiguous and open to interpretation. In contrast, LITTLE BIG MAN's narrator conducts the story, controls the viewer's understanding, provides a single point of view, and insists on one interpretation, attitude, and response to his story. (For a detailed discussion of this film, see Chapter 7.)

Another example of a narrator appears in THE PRINCESS BRIDE (1988) in which a wry old man, played by Peter Falk, reads a fairy tale to his ailing grandson and the fantasy images unfold under his voice. The child's voice, as he worries over the story's outcome or disagrees with its progress, interrupts from time to time. At each interruption the images switch back from the story to the sickroom where grandfather and grandson argue a bit about the way the narrative should go. When the grandfather returns to the reading, some of the images are "re-run" as he goes back to where he left off, his voice sometimes blending with the voice of a character repeating dialogue within the story. The story-book reading frames the action-adventure of the main story. The narrator is clearly telling the story from a position "off-screen," but when he appears on-screen he becomes a participating character.

In THE MAGNIFICENT AMBERSONS (1942), the voice of the narrator, Orson Welles, introduces the story and the characters in such a way that they respond to his disembodied voice. Once he has "set the story in motion," his voice does not intervene again until near the end when, with the weighty intonations reminiscent of the all-knowing narrator of the documentaries, he exposes the full significance of the main character's unfortunate situation. The director Welles ends the film with a *reflexive* or self-referential gesture: after introducing all the actors through cameos, he identifies himself as the narrator but shows only a picture of a microphone—a playful representation of his experience in radio and also of the all-knowing, all-powerful authorial voice.

Narration in Documentaries

In documentaries, a "disembodied" voice providing a "message of truth" came to be called the "Voice-of-God" style. Today, the use of this all-knowing, authoritative voice has fallen into some disfavor, especially among politically sensitive filmmakers who are aware of their power as the controllers of information. Recent documentary filmmakers have avoided the voice-over, preferring to let interviews or live action "tell the story," or letting on-screen interviews become voice-over narration when the images shift from the speaker to the subject of the interview. In a recent work by Pat Ferrero, HEARTS AND HANDS (1987), the voice-over narration consists of objective information combined with selections from the autobiographical writings, diaries, and letters of six historical women. Meanwhile the images document the locales of their lives and work; the artifacts—photographs and mementos—they saved; and the quilts they made, wrote about, and cherished.

Some documentary filmmakers have chosen to take a **self-reflexive** approach to their material. (*A "reflexive work" is like a mirror reflecting the subject—films about filming, for example or the place of the filmmaker.*) In the work of Chris Marker (THE KOUMIKO MYSTERY, 1965; SANS SOLEIL 1985), the narrator speaks in the first person but questions himself, acknowledging his own biases and intentions with respect to the film images. The "self-reflexive" perspective always

A

B

Figure 42 A. Hearts and Hands (d. Pat Ferrero, 1987). A quiltmaker and her children pose for a portrait in front of one of her quilts. (Courtesy of Thos K. Woodard Antiques.)
Figure 42 B. Hearts and Hands. A detail from a quilt made before the Civil War by a Quaker woman committed to the abolition of slavery. Her home in Pennsylvania was a stop on the Underground Railway—an organization that helped slaves escape from the South.

reminds the viewer that the material has been *interpreted* by the filmmaker.

The Vietnamese documentary filmmaker Trinh T. Minh-ha extends Marker's "self-reflexivity" and develops her own perspective on the notion of the voice-over narrator. In her film NAKED SPACES: LIVING IS ROUND (1986), she uses not one but three unseen female narrators, each of whom establishes a separate and distinct level of meaning carried in her *voice*, in her use of language, her intonation, accent, and timbre. Trinh's documentaries speculate on and experiment with ethnographic and documentary form and narration, pushing the forms to their limit.

In a twist on both the fictional narrators and the documentary "Voice-of-God" narrators, the fiction film NAKED CITY (1948) begins with the voice of Mark Hellinger, the film's producer, introducing himself as Mark Hellinger, the film's producer. In the course of the story he talks to the characters (although they don't respond to him); speaks for them; leaves room for them to speak their thoughts in their own voice-overs. Ultimately he sets himself up as all-knowing, judging the main character's actions and persistently directing the way the story is to be viewed, in another version of the powerful author/director. The relation to the documentary narrator reinforces the "truth" of the subject.

There are many possible strategies of narration, almost as many as there are films that choose to use the device. In every case, narrators *influence* interpretation of the images "under" their voice by means of the content they are providing and details of tone, accent, inflection. But the narrating voice-over, whether it attaches to a character eventually seen as part of the story or is disembodied, is only one of the narrators in a film. It is essential to recognize that the camera, although not "telling" in words, is the main narrator. The camera, *presenting* the images in a specific order and from a particular *point of view*, is always creating certain associations and so can be said to "tell" the story alongside any voice on the sound track.

Sound Effects

Sound effects refer to *all sounds that are not dialogue, narration or music*—everything from the tweet of a bird or the slam of a car door or ordinary street noises to the most fantastic creations of the supernatural and the extra-terrestrial. Whether they are recorded "live" or created by electronic or mechanical devices, a great deal of artistry, craft, thought, and care go into their creation and use.

Producing sound effects has become so complex over the years that it requires specialists, called **sound designers**. Real noises, recorded with a microphone do not necessarily sound like either our experience or our expectation of them. One sound engineer explained that, for example, recording ocean waves breaking on a beach results in a hissing sound rather than a crashing roar; it turns out that waves can be more convincingly produced by spraying water from a large hose onto gravel. Movie audiences are quite familiar with and accept as real, noises that do not sound like "the real thing." The most obvious examples are the sounds of a gunshot or a fist fight which, in any case, most people have heard *only* in the movies. The dull thuds heard in movies of earlier years (which may actually be close to the real sounds) have evolved through years of sound engineering, into the sharp, cracking smack used for the dramatic effect most filmmakers are after. The sound designer has the task of either *enhancing* some noises so they sound *more realistic than the real thing or completely fabricating noises when there is no "real thing,"* in science fiction worlds, for example, or nothing dramatic enough.

Except occasionally in animated cartoons, sound effects are rarely heard alone so sound designers must integrate the effects with realistic sounds and music. After the rough cut has been assembled, the sound designer constructs the sound track around it. The complex interweaving required by the "mix" of all the tracks and applied to the images, produces the associations, emotions, and tension every film requires.

Sound effects, real or electronically created, synchronous (with an image) or non-synchronous (as background), *heighten the illusion of the reality of the film world because hearing appropriate sounds corresponds to life experience.* Sounds *extend* the space of the frame. **Ambient** or **background sound** is not connected to specific visible sources but is necessary to the believability of the world of the story. It "creates" and defines locations, provides information about place, characters, and actions and contributes to the visual experience.

For a long time, the emphasis in the film industry has been on realism so sound effects are used to enhance realistic environments. However, sound effects have been used *expressively* for symbolic and "artistic" effect. Hitchcock and Welles, among others, have mixed realistic sound with its expressive use. Some modern films also use it symbolically. BRAZIL (1986) and MISHIMA (1985) use both image and sound in an artistic way. In THE SERPENT'S EGG (1972), Ingmar Bergman created a story around an unacknowledged and unnamed sound that comes to dominate the psychological levels of the lives of the characters.

Real or created sound is a powerful source of meaning. Just as different types of music, applied to the same image, change the reading of and response to that image, different sounds can change the mood of an image from ominous, to lively, to sad, to comical, to exciting. Whatever effect is intended, the sound designer has a complex task, balancing realism and expression.

Conclusion

In this chapter we have introduced a few of the many complex issues of *sound* in film. Filmmakers and their sound designers manipulate sounds like painters who mix their own colors, working them until they achieve the desired tones and intensities. But since the film industry has relied upon realism, sound, like other elements we have mentioned, is often considered most "successful" when the audience takes it for granted and does not especially notice it. Above all, it must not detract from the film's content. While the industry's "realist aesthetic" in general limits the possibility of creating imaginative and personally expressive sound, to a certain extent MTV's popular rock videos (the legacy, perhaps, of the 1960's experimental film movement) have liberated music and visuals. Through them many viewers have become familiar with and accept non-realistic, "surrealistic" images and sound.

Although most commercial feature films continue to be highly realistic (even when the subject is fantasy or science fiction), major theatrical releases increasingly incorporate radical and experimental devices in narrative, sound effects, music, and imagery. Movies like PINK FLOYD-THE WALL (1982), REPO MAN (1984), DESPERATELY SEEKING SUSAN (1985), CHOOSE ME (1984), and TRUE STORIES (1986), among other "alternative" movies, have become acceptable to a wider audience than might have been expected through the "visual training" rock videos provide.

Although we may think of film sound as secondary to the film image, actually both must work together to make meaning. The filmmaker weaves an intricate fabric of words, music, and sound effects around the images and invites us to make sense of the result. The viewer always *receives and interprets* sounds and relies on them as a guide to reading and responding to the images they accompany.

CHAPTER 6
Composition and Structure

To make a coherent film, camera and editing techniques are used to compose and structure the material to produce meaning. **Composition** and **structure** are related to each other; *both concern artistic arrangement and refer to the assembling of parts to form an organic whole.* However, in film they do not describe precisely the same artistic conceptions.

The word **composition** most accurately describes the *arrangement of visual elements in the shot* while **structure** applies to the *arrangement of narrative, informational, or visual elements into sequences.* In both fiction and non-fiction film, *each single shot is composed visually in the space of the frame; a sequence of shots is then structured, organized, and constructed over the time of the work.*

Composition and structure are important in all the arts but in the *"still"* arts—painting, sculpture, graphics, engraving, photography—composition is of primary importance. The artist executes the work by arranging the elements within the space of the canvas, or the stone, or the frame, or the paper, to produce balance and harmony. In what are called the *"time arts,"* the artist must consider, along with the composition of each shot, the overall structure of the larger work. By "time arts," in this book, we mean video and cinema, although music, dance, and performance art are normally included in the category as well since they, too, are *experienced over time.*

The *choices* the artist makes in selecting the arrangement of visual elements within the frame, come out of aesthetic traditions that in European-influenced cultures date back to the 16th century Renaissance and specifically to principles of *classical composition*. Currently, a reconsideration of these classical rules is taking place among artists and theorists. In other cultures with long artistic traditions of their own, the conception of space and the decisions made about the work of art have always been essentially different from classical western notions. Although there are many complex issues to consider, we are defining the principles in this chapter as those that have governed dominant western traditions in film.

Classical Composition

Since the Renaissance, artists have studied and applied the principles of **classical composition**. They have also periodically rebelled against those rules, exploring new avenues of expression and new directions in representation, but the principles remain the foundation upon which the visual aesthetic tradition of the Europe-centered world rests. *Classical composition creates a place for the viewer in relation to the blank space that is the canvas, the paper, or the screen; that place leaves room for the spectator whose point of view depends, in turn, on the visualization of perspective* (see fig. 43).

Figure 43. My Darling Clementine (d. John Ford, 1946). In this still, the space "left" for the spectator to fill is easy to spot—facing Wyatt Earp—while the eyeline direction of the characters shows that the bullets came from screen right.

Perspective

For a time, European-influenced artists were preoccupied with representing the world as it "is," with reproducing "reality"; that is, with making a picture "look exactly like" its subject. But truly reproducing "reality" is impossible so just producing the *illusion* of reality has had to be sufficient. For example, **artificial perspective** *creates the impression of three-dimensional space on a two-dimensional surface and, as a consequence, produces the illusion of depth*; the viewer perceives it as "natural." After its discovery, it became the basic principle of classical composition in drawing and painting.

To create perspective, the artist draws the subject—people and objects—often in relation to the *line of the horizon* (which is usually at the half way point on the canvas) and in relation to a *vanishing point* or *points. Figures meant to be distant are drawn smaller than those meant to be closer.* This is called **linear perspective** (see fig. 44). (By contrast, in Far Eastern art, figures in the background may be as large as those in the foreground because sometimes, to diminish a person's size in a drawing may suggest diminished respect for them.)

In another way to create perspective, called **aerial** or **atmospheric perspective**, the artist draws *closer objects in greater detail than distant ones which are in softer tones with the outlines more blurred* (see figs. 45, 46). Objects and figures are also placed in *overlapping planes* so that the closer ones partially block the distant ones from view. All these techniques used together create the *illusion* of three dimensions.

Before the development of perspective in the mid-fifteen hundreds, harmony and balance in a painting depended almost completely on the arrangement of figures and objects on the flat plane of the canvas. Their relative importance as subject matter determined both their placement and the size and detail with which they were drawn. For example, the Virgin Mary, holding the Christ child, was always of greater importance than the peasant kneeling at her feet; in paintings of that subject, the figures of the Virgin and Child were placed in the center, drawn large and detailed while the secondary figures were placed nearer the frame edges, drawn smaller and in less detail. After the discovery of perspective, the proportionate representation of objects and figures—large in the lower part of the canvas or foreground, smaller in the central part, or middleground, and smallest in the top part or background—became the accepted way to *represent* the scene and, therefore, the accepted way to *read* it.

Figure 44. **Mishima** (d. Paul Shrader, 1985). Linear perspective. A careful balance of the figures and the stylized set into which they are placed emphasize the depth of the frame, all the way to the vanishing point, which is blocked by the main figure facing forward. Greater depth to the frame is suggested by the horizon line and the sweep of the clouds.

Figure 45. Letter from an Unknown Woman (d. Max Ophuls, 1947). The line of snow running at a diagonal in the middleground marks a division between the foreground in sharp focus and the background in soft focus and soft grays. An example of aerial perspective giving great depth to the frame.

Composition: Space

The word **composition** pertains to the *deliberate organization of any work of art*. It comes from the Latin word for "putting together," and is defined as *"the arrangement of the parts of a work of art to form a unified, harmonious whole."* Studies in the psychology of perception have shown that the viewer tries to find harmony and balance in visual compositions; if s/he cannot, s/he feels anxiety and tension. Filmmakers always manipulate the harmony and disharmony of compositional elements to produce meaning within the film text and a range of responses in the viewer.

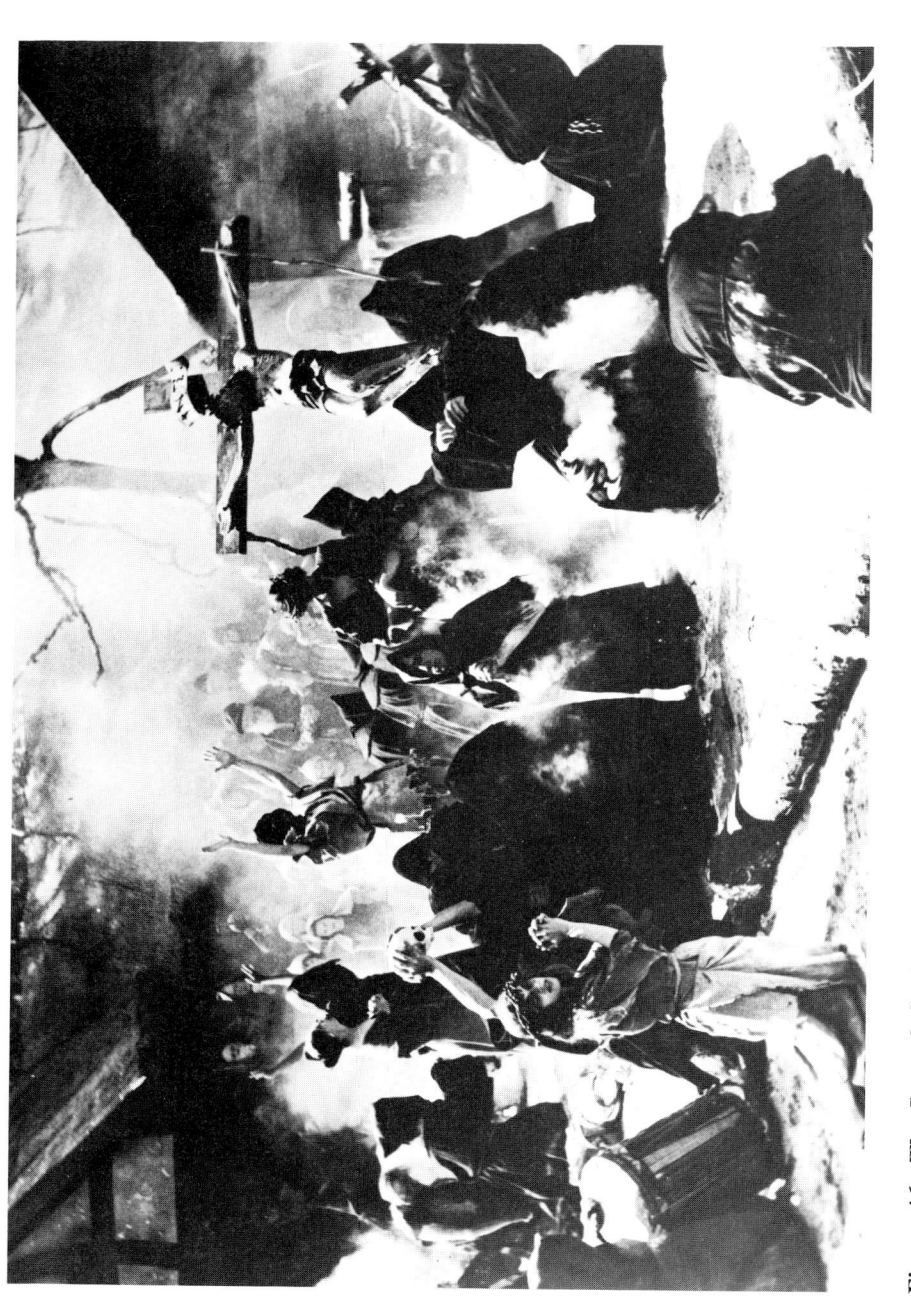

Figure 46. The Seventh Seal. The composition in the frame calls attention to the main point of interest in the middleground–the crucifixion. Repetition of the graphic element of the cross would normally lend harmony to the space in the frame. Here each of the cross designs is twisted, producing tension instead. Two characters are looking away from the central point of the frame, back toward the spectator. "Aerial perspective" produced partly by the smoke suggests a greater background area.

Graphic Elements of Composition

Another element in classical composition is **graphic design**, that is, the *arrangement of forms and shapes in a frame or picture-space*. The human eye is always immediately attracted to the *center* of any marked-out space. If the artist places a prominent figure in the background or adds a distinct color or a brightly lit object to the middleground, or adds movement in an otherwise still scene, then that area will become dominant. Otherwise, the center of the frame is most important and reserved for the most important information (see fig. 48).

After a first glance at the center of the image, and in the absence of other clues, those who read words from left to right will tend to read pictures in the same way, from left to right. For European influenced cultures, that eye movement gives priority to design elements located on the left of the frame over those on the right; in other cultures other areas would dominate. All these elements—graphic design, the priority of left over right and of the top over the bottom of the frame—along with size, volume, color, brightness, and movement may be used for *symbolic effects* while producing *visual pleasure* through the composition.

Composition in Film: The Frame

Filmmakers have had access to all forms of art; many have studied classical composition and principles of graphic design and incorporated them into the composition of the film image. All directors have recognized—at times intuitively, at times consciously—the ways in which composition in the frame affects the meaning of the shot. Sergei Eisenstein, for one, was convinced that **symmetrical compositions**, *centered, static, circular or angular forms*, convey a sense of balance, of harmony, even of stability while **asymmetrical compositions**, *off-center elements, unbalanced arrangements of objects, diagonal forms*, generate tension, anxiety, and excitement (see figs. 47 and 49).

A shot in which activity and objects spill over the edges of the frame, or one in which a moving camera seems to be "hurrying to catch up" with the action, works to reinforce the realism of the scene because it suggests that there is more "going on" than the camera can capture—that the events are not staged for the camera. Sometimes a director, Antonioni in ECLIPSE (1962), for example, will deliberately choose an "uncomposed" composition to suggest the impossibility of actually depicting reality. The objects and characters are not arranged in neatly

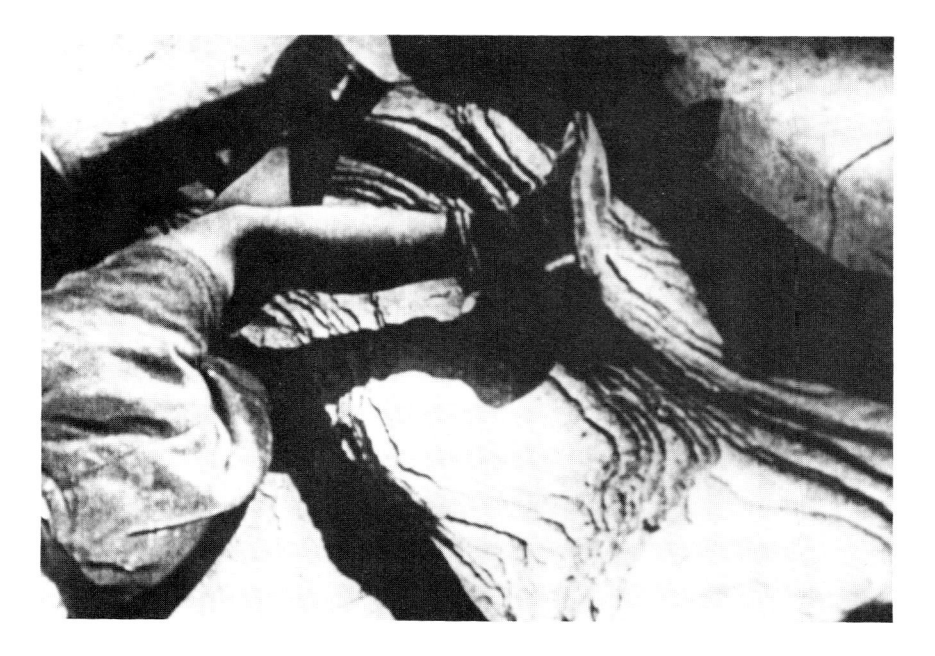

Figure 47. The Battleship Potemkin. The Odessa Steps sequence. Eisenstein preferred the dynamism of asymmetrical composition because it conveyed his view of a world in ferment and underlined his commitment to radical filmmaking. Here a child lying wounded on the steps extends out of frame disturbing the balance of the composition. The tension of the asymmetry is intensified by the cross-movement of people's feet as they stumble over him.

balanced places in the frame. Gillo Pontecorvo also has used "loose" composition to convey the hectic, unplanned quality of a recorded situation *as though* there were no time to compose, because "life was going by too fast" in THE BATTLE OF ALGIERS (1965) (see fig. 50).

Composition in Depth

Composition of a single film image—the shot—depends almost entirely on the set-up (placement of camera and lights), but it involves more than just the horizontal and vertical dimensions of the screen or frameline. Composition in film must take **depth** into consideration and filmmakers always compose the frame with this third "illusory" dimension in mind. How do they go about this process? The camera records ac-

Figure 48. The Grapes of Wrath (d. John Ford, 1940). John Ford preferred symmetrical compositions that depict a world of order, tradition, and stability. Here, a strong diagonal is formed by the Joad family, perched in descending order on the back of the truck, their gazes converging on Tom Joad (Henry Fonda in dark clothes). The handshake and the neighbor's uplifted face enclose the frame. Ma Joad (Jane Darwell), on the left, evens out the composition. The framing suggests a balance between anxiety and hope.

Figure 49. 2001: A Space Odyssey. A set using perfect symmetry for a balanced composition.

tion that has been arranged in three dimensions and then the filmed material is projected onto a two-dimensional screen. Because the actual filming records real space, a certain illusion of three-dimensionality will be automatically captured but, especially when certain constructed decors are used, the illusion is often incomplete. In such cases, the arrangement of people and objects becomes important in order to enhance or diminish the effect of realistic, three-dimensional space. Overlapping of planes, layering and backlighting of subjects, arranging of the subjects along a vanishing point, and lighting of the background, are all used regularly to enhance three-dimensionality. They are especially important in films that use sets with painted backdrops, or rear screen projection, or miniatures.

As we pointed out in Chapter 2, the camera lens itself can also affect the depth of the image, either flattening it out or intensifying it. The telephoto lens flattens out the natural depth of a set or location while the wide-angle lens will intensify it, especially in a location where actors and objects can be arranged in the **three planes**, *foreground, middleground and background*. Lights "model" or bring out the actors' features, add volume to their bodies and to objects around them, and separate them from the background. Then when the image is *projected onto a wide, slightly curved screen*, the maximum impact of *artificial perspective* is achieved and the shot looks three-dimensional.

Even in movies that are supposedly "strictly realistic," filmmakers often deliberately manipulate information, minimizing background and depth to concentrate on details. The background may be eliminated in a close-up of a face or an important object or may be shot out of focus or in *pulled focus* (the image is initially sharp but gradually goes out of focus except for a detail)—a face in the crowd, or a gun in an assassin's hand, or a letter in a jilted lover's hand. But in most feature films, the realistic space created by artificial perspective serves as a foundation and holds the (imaginary) world of the story together (see fig. 51).

Composition and Mise en Scene

Composition arranges on the flat surface of the screen what *mise en scene* arranges in depth: people and objects in front of the camera. Both composition and *mise en scene* require the director and cinematographer to design shots and place the camera in order to provide the desired effect. That effect may depend on secondary meanings. Shapes and forms often carry the secondary meanings: for example, *circles* are a traditional literary and visual form and when used either as a graphic element or in

Figure 50. The Killing Fields. (d. Roland Joffe, 1984). Loose or "uncomposed" composition shows the spill of action beyond the limits of the frame. While action occurs in the foreground, middleground and background, the bars (out of focus) in the extreme foreground form a barrier, trapping the running figures. The audience is, figuratively, separated from the fleeing group. In the still, the main character, Dith Pran, is neatly outlined in the center of the frame but in the film, the scene is one of movement and near chaos.

Figure 51. My Darling Clementine. In this deep focus shot, in spite of the weight provided by the line of men at the bar, the exact center of the frame is between Victor Mature and Ward Bond whose eyeline directions are exactly opposed. The balance in the frame is shifted by the walking stick, overhead lantern, and light on the rear wall to center attention on Henry Fonda.

Figure 52. Mise En Scene and Blocking. The actors, space, props, and decor are all carefully set up in front of the camera. The elements are "choreographed" to work with the choreographing of the can-can being shot by the camera on a crane. Note the production assistant holding the slate that marks the take number, standing in front of the dancers.

the movement of the camera, they might establish the *cyclical nature or endlessness* of a narrative situation (see fig. 53). Venetian blind *shadows* may resemble bars to *symbolize or foreshadow prison or entrapment*, as in many thrillers (see fig. 54). *Darkness and light* may divide the decor in a frame or a person's face and suggest the split between *good and evil*. *Distortions* of space and chaotic framing may *symbolize dislocation or anxiety*, as in MEAN STREETS (1973).

All these elements determine the viewer's response to the composition of the image: dynamism and balance, size, shape, color, brightness, placement in the frame, and movement (see fig. 52).

Figure 53. 2001: A Space Odyssey. This wide-angle shot of the set is based on symmetry and the circle. The position of the characters parallel to the normal horizon line in composition suggests the difference between earth-bound physical limitations and the freedom of outer space.

119

Composition and Screen Size

When composing a shot, the director must consider **screen size and shape** because they set the *limits of the field of vision* to be filled. The composition is modified depending on the proportions of the screen. For the first fifty years of production, the screen was a standard rectangle with an **aspect ratio**, *the ratio of height to width* of 1.33:1, that is, one and one third times wider than it was high. (It was called the "Academy" ratio because the Academy of Motion Pictures Arts and Sciences favored it.) The Academy screen size and shape was thought to offer nearly perfect proportions for well-balanced composition and was used for all production. CASABLANCA, THE GRAPES OF WRATH and THE BATTLESHIP POTEMKIN were all composed according to the Academy ratio.

Then in the 1950's, TV began to develop as a medium and also began to use this ratio, the "Golden Mean," as it was also sometimes called. But when TV began to cut into the "audience share" of the movies, film directors, trying to distinguish their "product" from the intruder's, took shelter behind the difference between the "big screen" and the "little box" and moved into extremes of big screen production. To make the best use of the wide screen, the industry developed Todd-AO and Cinemascope, with aspect ratios of 2.2:1 and 2.35:1, screens over twice as wide as they were high.

Initially, wide screen formats were reserved for big-budget, spectacular extravaganzas, but as the film industry adjusted to the permanent presence of TV, the wider screen became the standard format for almost all feature production. Currently, the industry operates with two aspect ratios, both wide screen: the average, a width just under twice its height (1.85:1) and the other with a width nearly three times its height (2.7:1).

The changes in screen size have affected both production and composition. First of all, the great screen width increases the impression of depth and lends itself to the use of deep focus and composition in depth. Secondly, the traditional sequences of editing (long shot to medium shot to close-up) and the master shot with its close-up inserts, do not work well on the wide screen; filling a large screen with a single close-up is difficult and may be unnecessary since details can often be presented through compositions using *deep focus*. Third, a larger image size lends itself to spacious locations and elaborate *mise en scene* in comparison to the more confined frames of the Academy ratio and the TV screens.

These days, producers are making films with television rights in mind, and since the TV screen cannot tolerate wide screen composition, directors emphasize **centralized composition**—*placing all important information, action, and figures at the center of the frame.* Facing the inevitable transfer to the small screen, camera lenses are marked to show the cinematographer exactly what part of the composition will remain in the TV frame after the film is converted, ensuring minimal loss. The trend to television and video tape bears on many aspects of film production and will be discussed further in Chapter 8.

Dynamic Composition

The principles of classical composition devised for the still arts must be modified for film and video, which depend upon movement. **Motion**, either *of the camera or the characters*, is an important way of creating a *dominant point of interest within the frame* and will inevitably *change the balance of the frame composition*. The power of the image in films comes not from one "frozen" image but from what can be called **dynamic composition**, *the composition of a number of graphic elements in motion.* The way movement changes these elements and affects their arrangement may be illustrated by an example from Orson Welles' TOUCH OF EVIL (1958).

In the opening sequence, a close-up shot, lit in dramatic low key, shows hands planting a bomb in the trunk of a car. The camera tracks back slightly to show a couple getting into the car. As they drive out of the parking lot on one side of a building, the camera tracks along on the other side, picking them up as they pull out into the street. The camera continues to track back, revealing an entire town, lively with traffic and people. Along the way it picks up another couple, Mike Vargas (Charleton Heston) and his wife, Susan (Janet Leigh). The camera stays with them, always keeping the car with the bomb in it in the frame. In this single shot, camera movement has reversed the dominant points of interest: the activities of the couple in medium range have suddenly become more interesting than those in the close shot.

Dynamic composition *within* the shot is important but composition takes place *between* shots as well. In Chapter 4 we discussed screen direction, matching action, matching of graphic elements, camera movement, and dissolves, and pointed out their use as transitional links. These devices are important in composition because the connections must also be planned and considered ahead of time in the composition of the shot. Matching devices not only help the images glide invisibly from one shot to the next, they contribute to dynamic composition. since all transitional

Figure 54. Touch of Evil (d. Orson Welles, 1958). "Film noir" lighting. Shadows of the venetian blinds on the wall, strong key light on Vargas' (Charleton Heston) face. Detective Hank Quinlan's (Orson Welles) eyes are masked by the brim of his hat, suggesting, along with his slovenly appearance, his deceit borne out in the course of the car bomb investigation. Here, at a turning point in the film, Vargas, a narcotics agent, discovers Quinlan planting a stick of dynamite as false evidence in a suspect's house.

devices, whether used to create continuity or discontinuity, affect composition. The filmmaker can compose a seemingly **continuous imaginary space**, one that *looks and "feels" three-dimensional*, by using *artificial perspective* and *deep focus (all planes of the frame kept in focus)* to help achieve three-dimensionality, and by combining shots to produce cohesive space that could be "mapped out."

For example, if in shot #1 a character is standing on a street corner in the center of the frame and then starts across the street toward what is the bottom left-hand corner of the screen, the viewer would expect to see her reach the other side of the street in shot #2, moving in the same direction. In other words, she would enter the frame of shot #2 in the upper right hand corner, again headed toward the lower left corner. The direction of the movement makes the shots flow smoothly and *indicates that the new space extends from the preceding area.* If the character were to enter shot #2 from the upper left hand corner, not only would continuity be violated but the viewer would be disoriented.

Documentary and experimental filmmakers sometimes use dynamic composition to create *connections* between information and meaning. They tie separate concepts together by using a version of what Eisenstein called "**intellectual montage**," his term for the *joining of two images that contain differing, contrasting, or seemingly unrelated information to make an abstract idea concrete.* This construction, according to Eisenstein, forces the viewer to look for a way to associate and connect the two separate images. A famous example from his own work appears in OCTOBER (1928). He inserts an image of a peacock between two shots of the politician Alexander Kerensky. His idea was to point out Kerensky's vanity and swagger. Whether the connection is accessible to people unfamiliar with the historical figure, or whether these kinds of abstract connections are *ever* readily accessible, remains in question.

Peter Davis attempted a similar connection in his documentary HEARTS AND MINDS (1974). By juxtaposing images of the war in Viet Nam with those of a football game he establishes a visual comparison between the brutality of football and the savagery of war. Viewers may have understood the comparison and either accepted or rejected it on ideological grounds. It is also possible that some were confused by the cross-cutting between the jungles of Southeast Asia and a football field since the relation between the two locations—however well developed through matching movement, graphic forms, and slogans—was only a theoretical one.

Feature films rely on dynamic composition, especially in sequences that show action occurring in several locations or that disrupt the sense of coherent space for dramatic purpose—in crowd scenes or war stories. *Dynamic composition organizes movement within the individual shot* and also *creates continuous space across shots.* It most often carefully locates people, places, and objects in relation to one another (even though they may never appear together in the same shot). But it may also be used to generate a deeper level of complex meaning by associating or contrasting different images. Dynamic composition, because it connects shots with one another, introduces the element of time and leads us to the other issue under discussion: **structure**.

Structure: Time

The composition of visual material within the shot and between shots organizes space; **structure** *organizes time.* However, this does not mean that composition is *only visual* and structure is *only temporal*. On the contrary, the composition of each single frame, while *primarily* visual, must also relate to the whole work, and the structure of a film, while *primarily* temporal, must be included in the visual imagery as well. The structure emerges as it unfolds over the time of the work, sometimes as a "story"—a "narrative"—sometimes in essay form, sometimes in visual form.

Visual and narrative structures are based for the most part on **repetition** (with variation). Certain shots are regularly repeated to keep viewers oriented within the imaginary space of the action (establishing shots, reaction shots shot-reverse-shot patterns). Dialogue may be repeated; angles and lighting may be repeated; scenes may recur. Repetition is often used for emphasis and clarification. In documentaries the location of a character or an object may be shown several times to explain the situation being discussed. In fiction films, repetition, in the form of the "motif" which may be either visual or aural, may be used to develop symbolic significance. In experimental films especially, repetition of any element, narrative, informational, or visual, creates and contributes to meaning and rhythm.

Fiction and Non-fiction Film

It is useful to classify films *not* as narrative and non-narrative, but as **fiction** and **non-fiction** forms. Any type of film can be narrative, that is, *tell a story*, but the story may be imaginary, in which case it is fiction, or "true," in which case it is non-fiction. Any thread of information which links events together by time-sequence is narrative. The sentence "the Queen died and the King died" is a naming of events; the sentence "the Queen died *and then t*he King died" is a chronological linking of events. But to really make it a story there must be cause and effect: "*Because* the Queen died the King died." Newspaper stories, TV news reports, and some advertisements are almost always presented as narratives—using dramatic elements and stating or implying sequence and cause. In fact news reports often use an approach like old "cliffhangers" or TV soap operas use, to present events even as serious as the Chernobyl nuclear disaster; they create suspense so the audience will "tune in to find out what happens next."

Fiction, documentary, and many experimental films rely to some extent on narrative structure. If a filmmaker chooses not to use narrative as the organizing principle of a film, the only other structural basis s/he can use is formal: that is, the visual patterning of graphic elements ("forms") is elaborated for sensory, aesthetic, and emotional effect. But film, by its visual nature, must usually *combine* narrative and visual elements.

Structure: Narrative Film

Most of us are familiar with conventional narratives after years of watching movies, TV situation comedies, soap operas, dramatic serials, (and reading novels). If we analyze narrative films in the same way we would a novel, short story, or drama, we might find a useful approach. Film resembles the written narrative forms in certain ways but narrative is translated, through images, into another medium. Films are a unique form of representation, requiring different conceptual foundations as well as the addition of a technical dimension; but narrative films, like other story-telling forms, depend on **plot, setting, characterization, and imagery**.

The plot arranges the order of the events of the story. The order may be chronological, that is move the events forward in sequence. The order may "flashback" or events may occur simultaneously. **Setting**, both the *time and the place of the action,* is crucial. Location and time of day or season can be as important for meaning as a particular historical moment. **Characterization** shows *development, changes, and motivation of each individual as well as the interactions among them.* **Imagery** goes beyond the fact that films are based on pictures. The term *"imagery"* refers to the *way the images are used—repeated or contrasted—and the way they become symbols of larger meaning* (see fig. 55).

Connections between an event that takes place in a particular place at a particular time and the *kinds* of people involved in the action, their personality or character traits, their relationships with themselves and each other, make it possible to perceive the meaning, or larger significance of otherwise disconnected elements. "Goodness" equals a set of behaviors some of which we see on the screen, but the idea of "good" will vary according to the cultural and historical context. For example, is Will Kane (in HIGH NOON) "good" and brave because he stands up to the Frank

Figure 55. The Grapes of Wrath. In this shot from the classic narrative film adapted from John Steinbeck's famous novel, all the elements of the fiction are represented. The era of the Depression as setting, characterization in the person of the hero, and the theme of the break-up of families because of hard times are suggested by the image here of the characters in the mirror. Tom Joad (Henry Fonda) is both reflected in the mirror and separated from his family by its frame. The imagery literally *reflects* the themes.

Miller gang or is he self-serving, attempting to involve the townspeople in a personal fight against the gang's revenge? Is Holly Hunter's character in BROADCAST NEWS "good" because she does *not* marry either of her co-workers, or foolish? Is she full of integrity or full of pretense? The answer in both cases is a matter of how the character is presented through point of view.

As a result of our experience with stories, most of us have expectations of what a story should be. These develop, in part, because certain kinds of stories reappear again and again. (Another form of repetition.) Most narrative films fall into a *genre,* a story that contains predictable elements. Hollywood has relied on genres because a tried and true for-

Figure 56. Bonnie and Clyde (d. Arthur Penn, 1967). Easily recognizable as a gangster film but, because of its setting in the rural West during the Depression it also recalls the western and the '30's social commentary genres.

mula is less risky than something new and different. Genre stories are so familiar that we know what to expect from a film advertised as a western, a detective movie, a gangster film, a science fiction film, horror film, or a melodrama. In a western we expect to see, set in a particular time, horses, rifles, wide-open spaces; those elements would occur in "the generic western," although additional ones may also be included: sheepherders and cattlemen, ranchers and land developers, banks and robbers or trains and robbers. Anyone can think of specific "brand name" westerns. They include every type from THE LONE RANGER, through STAGECOACH, to SILVERADO and LITTLE BIG MAN. (See Chapter 7).

The western is one type of **adventure** story. These are typically set in colorful locations and involve the quest for a prize—knowledge, power, or wealth—danger, and triumph over obstacles. LAWRENCE OF

ARABIA (1962), NEVER CRY WOLF (1983); OUT OF AFRICA (1985) are recognizable examples of the basic adventure story. Audience familiarity with the genre means that it eventually lends itself to parodies and take-offs such as RAIDERS OF THE LOST ARC (1981), ISHTAR (1987), ROMANCING THE STONE (1984), among others.

The basic principle governing the structure of any genre film is *narrative repetition*. The plots are predictable, take place in appropriate places, and use familiar characters: cowboys and Indians battle it out in the wild west; gangsters commit crimes in cities; adventures take place in exotic lands with wild and daring heroes and determined, but often helpless heroines, etc. These days many movies are made that fall easily into these categories, although most in fact combine elements from many genres. For the most part, however, these films do little more than rework slightly the same old stories. They are "safe investments."

A small number of films do not fit so easily into genre categories mainly just because they are *not* based on formula. In these films, **themes** are shaped out of a delicate balance among the component parts. A handful of acknowledged "great" films belong to this group, among them CITIZEN KANE, THE TREASURE OF THE SIERRA MADRE (1948), the French films, THE RULES OF THE GAME (1939), THE GRAND ILLUSION (1937), CHILDREN OF PARADISE (1944), and the contemporary two-part work JEAN DE FLORETTE and MANON OF THE SPRINGS (1987). In these, the director fuses technical knowledge, content, and conceptual elements to make meaning. The films raise social, political, psychological questions but almost always relate stories that illustrate actual human experience. Their themes draw on ideas and images that are both individual and universal and so complex that the films defy conventions and limitations.

Structure: Documentary Film

The documentary film is an essentially non-fiction form which, at first glance, seems to use visuals and narrative only to present content. However, the name *documentary* covers a wide range of films, from non-fiction narratives to "rock docs," documentaries of rock music performances. Documentaries deal with events, issues, political situations, or a way of life, among an almost infinite number of subjects. Their primary goal is usually to inform rather than to "entertain" yet they must hold the audience's interest. Therefore, while they are not normally thought to concern themselves with the usual elements of fiction—storyline, plot,

Figure 57A. Dark Circle (d. Chris Beaver, Judy Irving, Ruth Landy, 1983). The issue: A government photo of a worker handling a plutonium button at the Rocky Flats Nuclear Weapons plant.(© Independent Documentary Group)

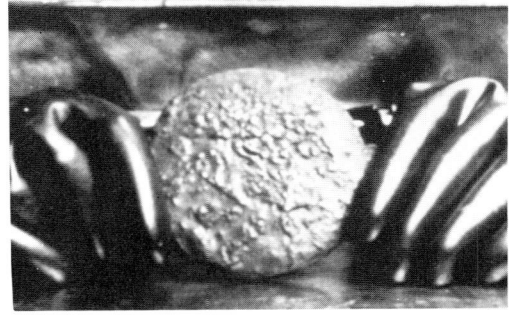

Figure 57B. Dark Circle. Documentation of group opposition to nuclear proliferation: Civil disobedience at the Diablo Canyon Nuclear Power plant in 1977. (© Karen Spangenberg)

Figure 57C. Dark Circle. The filmmakers' personal response: This photo, taken in Hiroshima the day after the bombing, shows the destruction and human suffering. The clouding and marks on the photo may be the result of exposure to radioactivity during the developing. (© Independent Documentary Group)

characters, dramatic conflict, suspense, climax, and resolution—the films are often organized around some of these elements and, in fact, sometimes develop a narrative around which they structure information or ideas. That is, they "tell a story," but not a fictitious story.

A BURDEN OF DREAMS (1982), a documentary by Les Blank, tells a true story about another filmmaker, Werner Herzog who, making his own narrative film (FITZCARRALDO) became so obsessed with the search for authentic detail that he risked human lives and the whole production. Blank chose to structure the documentary as a "story" of a "character" and it contains action, suspense, a climax, and a final resolution—"like" a narrative film. In this case, the documentary takes on the form of a *non-fiction narrative*.

On the other hand, a documentary filmmaker may choose to structure a film around interviews ("talking heads"), to let the people involved "tell their own stories." This type may also include elements associated with fiction: characterizations, personal histories, emotion, irony. Yet another type of structure would parallel the essay form in writing. Frederick Wiseman develops this kind of structure in his many films on social systems and institutions: HIGH SCHOOL (1968) and WELFARE (1956) among them.

Judy Irving and Chris Beaver, in their film DARK CIRCLE (1983), combine first person, voice-over narration with information and a political statement about nuclear proliferation. The structure combines the informative essay with personal response to a global problem. A different combination is found in HEARTS AND HANDS (1987) by Pat Ferrero. That documentary, about the quiltmaking craft in the history of the United States, pulls together fragments of women's autobiographies, diary entries, and letters, matching them to the film images to make a "patchwork" of narrative and historical essay.

The documentary film is a form open to modification by imaginative and perceptive filmmakers. Because it is not a "commercial" form, both its subject matter and its methods tend to be more flexible than those of narrative fiction.

Structure: Experimental Film

It is impossible to list a single set of characteristics or structural principles for experimental cinema. By definition the **experimental cinema** locates itself at the *leading edge of artistic exploration, defying traditions, expanding the medium and its forms*. Theorists point out that experimental films share only the fact that they are are personal, unconventional statements. In fact, other terms for experimental film are "avant-garde" films, in English the vanguard, suggesting their place in the *forefront* of cinematic exploration; "alternative cinema," suggesting an *alternative* to the dominant industry, and "personal cinema," underlining the *individual vision* that goes into the creation of the films. In their use of visual forms they reject many of the usual conventions (which can make them somewhat inaccessible to the unprepared viewer). However, once we learn to recognize their structures—narrative and visual— these films, too, become understandable.

The notion of experimental is connected to historical time: what is considered "experimental" in one period may become completely acceptable, even "old hat," in another. For example, during his lifetime, Van Gogh was considered not only a radical but a bad artist; a hundred years later he is considered a genius. Almost every composer now considered great, from Beethoven to Debussy was considered radical during his lifetime. In rock music, Little Richard and Jimmy Hendrix were both considered too far out. Today all of these artists are all completely accepted.

Experimental film has had a parallel history to that of the mainstream. The position of these filmmakers has been that formulas, genres, and the demands of the market place inhibit the *art* of the medium. They make their films not for financial gain but because they want to explore the potential of the medium that they feel cannot be explored in commercial work. Their object is to make a contribution to the form and the art rather than to "entertain."

The fundamental organizing element of experimental films is usually their visual structure—often poetic, symbolic, or intuitive. Experimental films have been based on harmonic musical structures, visual design, and dream imagery, and a variety of other elements. However complex and inaccessible these films were originally, in many cases their structures, ideas, and techniques were eventually absorbed into the mainstream.

The structuring and unifying element, in purely visual films, is, once again, almost always repetition. Images, angles, lighting, shot length, many elements not always individually noticeable, recur, usually with some variation. Either a rhythmic or periodic pattern is created that produces a coherent whole. MESHES OF THE AFTERNOON (1947), according to its creator, Maya Deren, one of the important American experimental filmmakers of the '40's, was an attempt to capture and reproduce the way the mind elaborates and interprets experience. To cap-

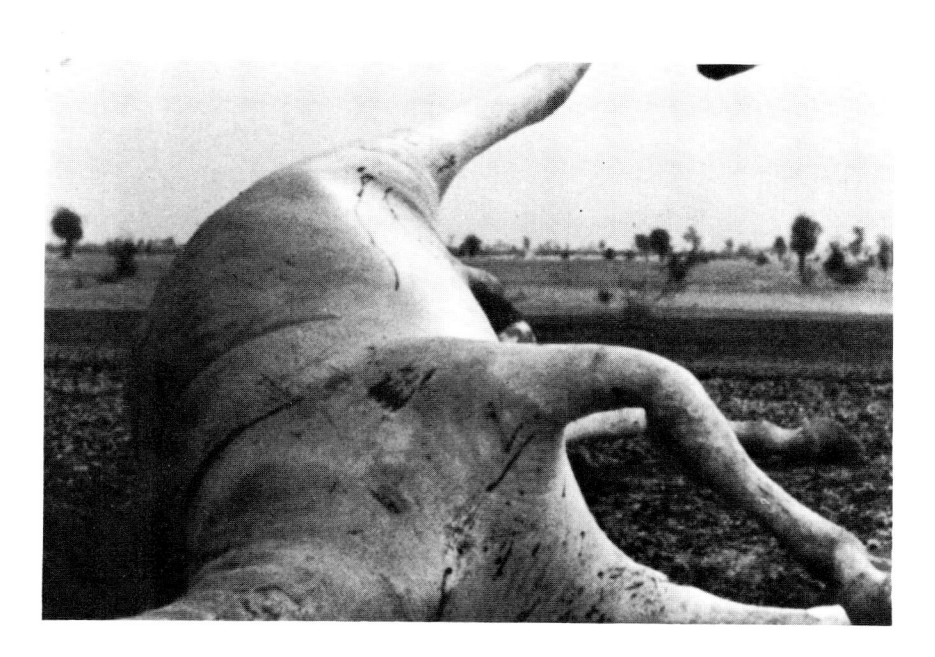

Figure 58. Reassemblage (d. Trinh T. Minh-ha, 1983). This experimental documentarian combines shots of a dead donkey into visual structure showing first the stillness of its feet, then this abstract composition of the animal's almost unrecognizable body. The donkey's death is not apparent until we see its head in the subsequent shot.

ture the workings of the mind, Deren used recurring visual motifs—a shrouded figure, objects—a key, a mirror, a telephone—represent the symbolic connections produced by memory and dreams.

The contemporary experimental filmmaker Karen Holmes's films use recurring shapes in different contexts to generate meaning. The movement of a walking figure in a landscape structures SAVING THE PROOF (1985). Here, the graphic elements of the shots are manipulated (through complex optical processes) by adding, subtracting, layering, and altering the images to order and unify the fragmented information. As we pointed out in the last chapter, sound is an important element in the work of experimental filmmakers—and Holmes is no exception—who use complex sound structures to support the complex visual structures.

Experimental films may be fiction or non-fiction, narrative or non-narrative. They might even be called "anti-fiction" or "anti-narrative" because they deliberately question the very foundations of those forms. The categories are never completely exclusive so while it is important to recognize the areas of narrative, documentary and experimental film and

Figure 59. Saving the Proof. Four separate images were layered to produce this image. Note the clear shape in the middle of the frame created by a travelling matte of the woman's body. The matte and all three figures move in different directions.

the division between fiction and non-fiction, actual practice often *combines* these forms. There are experimental documentaries (the work of Chris Marker, Trinh T. Minh-ha, and Chick Strand) and narrative documentaries (the work of Robert Flaherty, Les Blank, and Pat Ferrero); and there are experimental narratives (the work of Maya Deren, Mark Rapaport, Valie Export).

Conclusion

All of the possibilities of composition and structure are at the disposal of the filmmaker who wishes to tell stories, explore visual experience, or to comment on the *actual* social, historical, political and human situations of our world. Within the commercial film industry the range of structuring and composing possibilities has been considerably limited by the market for narrative film and the resulting tendency to stick to old and proven genres, themes, and character types. Nevertheless, as we will see in the next chapter, the combination of compositional elements and structuring strategies offers the filmmaker a rich resource for making meaning in film.

CHAPTER 7
Making Meaning

Films are a form of communication with a viewer and the purpose of all communication is to convey information. The purpose of making a film is to tell a story, to document an event, to investigate a situation, to persuade or convince, or to explore an idea. The competent filmmaker *creates* meaning; we must learn how to *extract* meaning.

How do filmmakers produce meaning? Filmmakers manipulate the materials and techniques available to them. They select the elements of *cinematography*, the angle, distance, lighting—the appropriate set-up for a particular kind of film. They *edit*, arrange sequences into a particular order; they *compose and structure* visual and narrative elements, imagery, setting, and characterization. At all times, the filmmaker must strike a balance between narrative form and visual representation.

The preceding chapters have concentrated on the technical and conceptual processes used to make films—camera techniques, lighting, set design, sound, acting, editing, structure and composition. *In this chapter we will look at the way the processes, worked together, produce meaning in the shot, in the sequence, and in the entire film.* To examine the results, we will concentrate, although not exclusively, on an **analysis** of the narrative film, LITTLE BIG MAN (1970), directed by Arthur Penn. The principles governing production of meaning, however, may be applied to any film.

Film as Language

Early theorists of editing compared film to language with the shot like a word and the sequence like a sentence. The theorists were not saying that shots were the *same* as words but that they were *like* words, that they work with each other to produce meaning the way words do in a sentence; words and shots gain meaning from the *context*. Sergei Eisenstein, who wrote extensively on all areas of film, proposed a theory based on this comparison to language. He said that *individual shots are only partial details of the whole and cannot stand alone.* He thought that shots work together to produce an *aggregate or cumulative* meaning—one which does not exist in any single shot but grows out from all the shots put together—again, a *context.* Understanding the material within the single shot and in the context makes it possible to "read" the meaning of the entire film. *Our understanding of each shot is affected by the shots that have preceded it* (and, Eisenstein would say, those that come after it since he assumed detailed study of the works). *The accumulation of material makes it possible to understand the film as a whole.*

The idea that the viewer understands film the way s/he understands language has gained some support over the years while quite sophisticated theories of the relation between language and film have continued to be applied to account for film's specifically *visual* quality—that is, the fact that it *shows* rather than *tells* information. It is widely accepted that films are carefully *constructed* and that they *show information* in such a way that *intended meanings are conveyed at several levels.*

One way to learn to "see" and "read" these various levels of meaning is to **analyze** the film, which as for any work of art, involves study and, in the case of film, several careful viewings. *The object is to break the work down into its component parts, to then look carefully at those parts—sequences and shots—and to place each into its larger context—shots within the sequence, the sequence within the whole film.* Through this kind of examination, the *interaction* among all the elements becomes clear. As we have come to recognize, **repetition**—of visual and narrative motifs, symbols, allusions—*is the foundation of all kinds of structure.* Out of the **structure** *meaning appears.* Finally, out of the *interaction among all the elements*, important **areas of thematic concern** emerge.

Underlying Meaning

Whether we realize it or not, *every experience is actually "full of meaning."* In fact, we spend most of our time either *making meaning ourselves (speaking or writing) or making sense of meanings others have produced (reading or viewing).* We live in a world full of **signs** that we must interpret in order to live—for example, *street signs* which give information about a city; different *traffic signs* tell drivers where to turn, how fast to go, and what road conditions to expect. *Traffic lights* are signs that tell them when to stop and when to go. By the same token, the *colors of the trees* signal the seasons; *smoke* is usually a sign of fire; *geological* *formations*, rocks, volcanic activity, and erosion patterns provide signs of the history of the earth (see fig. 60).

These are all recognizable as signs and depend on inanimate objects but people also signal feelings or thoughts, often involuntarily, which other people interpret. The *look on a person's face* may be a sign of either trustworthiness or unreliability; *gestures and posture* may indicate a mood. *Clothes* often relay messages about the wearer's economic and social status as well as taste. Even *food choices* can reveal character, class, and upbringing, and perhaps more. What if a person drinks diet Pepsi, Miller's or Heineken dark beer? Or eats "junk food," "California cuisine," or health food? What might these preferences suggest? We interpret these choices as signs of character that we understand depending on our personal experience (or sometimes on our exposure to advertising).

Signs are an important element in movies as well; film images contain a great deal of information and often represent activities we are familiar with in daily life. The filmmaker usually extends the meaning of

Figure 60. To the uninformed this picture looks like no more than an interesting pattern of rocks. But geologists can tell by studying them that there were once volcanos here; the streaks visible on the surfaces reveal that the area was later covered by glaciers. (Courtesy Dr. Raymond Pestrong)

the sign, *uses* it to give extra information, to produce visual and auditory *communication*, which, consciously or not, as "consumers of meaning" from birth, we interpret as we watch. For example, the filmmaker may convey a point or idea by using a certain lighting to emphasize a part of the image, by framing, by repeating an image or a sequence, or by editing. We perceive, "read," these single elements, note them and then, when they recur, we put the instances together to make sense of them. *They have become signs of some other meaning.*

Meaning in a shot, sequence, or the entire film occurs at two levels: the **literal level** and the **connotative level**. Both must be considered and analyzed to fully understand a film. Literal meaning is information that emerges from the object or word; connotative meaning is associative—feelings and ideas are linked mentally with the object or word; information is hinted at or implied and arises from the meaning we invest into the material.

Connotation

Figure 61. The "mushroom cloud" has become a cultural sign just since 1945. It goes beyond connotation and becomes a symbol of death, destruction, the end of the world, regardless of the specific context. The textual connotation in DARK CIRCLE (from which this shot comes) is not much different from that in "Dr. Strangelove" even though the *form* and *tone* of the two films are quite different. (© Independent Documentary Group)

Connotation, in turn, supplies meaning in two ways. The first depends on *cultural knowledge* and so can reasonably be called **cultural connotation**. The second way depends on the *meanings produced by the specific text* and can be called **textual connotation**.

Cultural connotation is based on the things everyone learns about society in general, people in that society, ways of living and behaving in that social group—in other words, *values, assumptions*, and *expectations*. Everything we do, think, say, believe, depends on cultural knowledge, on things learned since birth about how to get on in the world. Some part of this knowledge is individual—people have their own way of going about some things; however, a great deal more is cultural.

To give an example of cultural connotation, let's look at the word "coat." The object is usually used to keep a person warm. But just from seeing someone—say a clean-cut young man of about twenty-one—wearing a particular coat, we can guess quite a bit about him. If the coat happens to be a *knee-length black wool* overcoat and with it he's wearing white high-top Reeboks, faded black Levis, and a white shirt, the "outfit" *suggests* that he's "trendy," at least according to the popular fashions of college life in the western United States, in the late 1980's. But what if, instead of the coat, he is wearing a down parka? Or a "distressed-leather" flyer's jacket? Each of these different coats gives differing information about the wearer.

The *literal* meaning is that the coat is a garment. But immediately, all the *connotative* meanings arise, that is, the *implications*, the *meanings suggested* by the specific type of coat. A fashion magazine might interpret them this way: "campus cool" (overcoat), "ski-slope chic" (parka), "casually masculine" (leather). Most of us will even judge his character based largely on his choice of outfit—our response to what we "read" in the *sign* of the clothing. We might find him appealing because we expect him to be sophisticated, or athletic, or forceful and exciting. Or we might reject him: he's pretentious, part of "that ski-set," too macho.

It is often difficult to distinguish between *literal* and *connotative* meanings. But the literal information about an object, expression, scene or situation is often taken for granted while the connotative or underlying meaning seems to hold the real significance. Coats are not a bad example; advertisements endow clothes with the power to provide identity and produce prosperity—the slogans "dress for success" and "look like a million" promise success. The original, *literal* significance of the coat— it covers and warms—is dismissed. People have been known to spend an entire evening shivering because a warm coat didn't go with their outfit. For most of us it is not until we begin to shiver that the distinction between literal and connotative meaning becomes clear.

Everyone who has learned the ways of her/his own society recognizes behavior that is, for example, polite, considerate, and proper and does not confuse it with behavior that is rude, inconsiderate, and improper. That recognition depends on being able to *read* behavior and attitudes through other people's actions, gestures, and appearances. The viewer of a film reads behavior the same way. In HIS GIRL FRIDAY (1940), for ex-

Figure 62. Psycho. Janet Leigh's expression takes on significance because of the money she holds. She is conflicted and distressed. The specific textual connotation of guilt emerges from this shot's place in the film.

ample, the newspaper editor Walter Burns is *visibly* ungentlemanly and inconsiderate, in particular toward his former wife Hildy; in CASABLANCA, Rick is *visibly* disturbed by suddenly seeing his former love, Ilse. These behaviors have cultural connotations associated with them.

Textual connotation, while often based on cultural connotation, *emerges out of the organization of the work itself.* In a film (or in literature), themes, symbols, motifs, allusions, and implications are developed through the specific interaction of elements in the story or piece. Because these meanings emerge from the *text*, that is from the film itself and specifically from the way the images are organized into a meaningful structure, they are said to comprise *textual connotation.* For example, in CASABLANCA, the song "As Time Goes By" is heard several times as background music in orchestrated version (see fig. 32). When Ilse asks Sam to play it (and names it), he refuses and then reluctantly begins. The tune brings Rick over saying, "I thought I told you never to play that..."; he catches sight of Ilse. To this point the viewer has no idea of the significance of the song. Its meaning within the film is only "explained" later, implied during the flashback in which we learn that it was the song Sam played on the day of Rick and Ilse's last, fateful, meet-

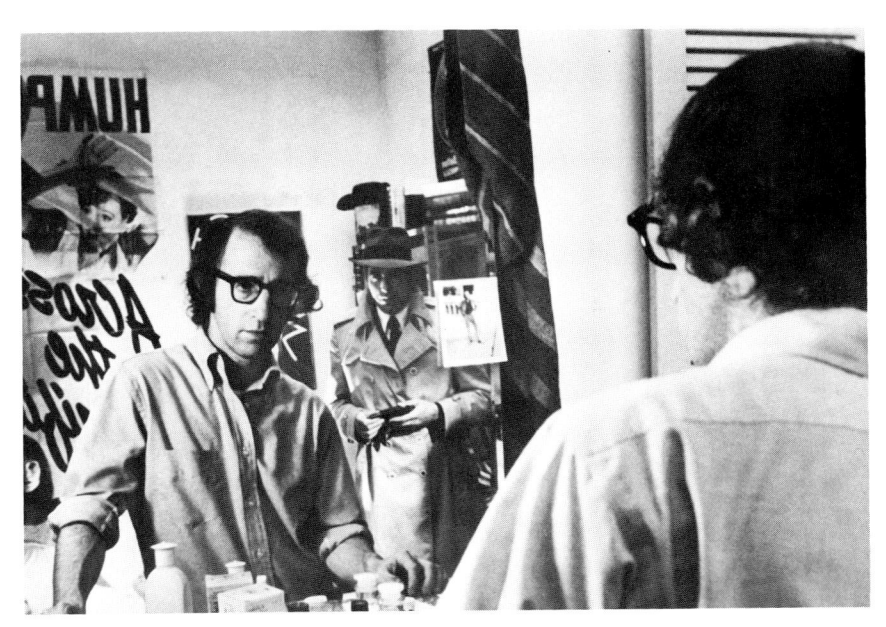

Figure 63. Play It Again, Sam (d. Woody Allen, 1972). "Bogart reappears" to counsel the protagonist in Woody Allen's homage to CASABLANCA.

ing before she "stood him up." The song takes on levels of meaning—it represents that last moment together, then the whole love affair, including Paris and innocent times before the war, extending to represent Rick's never verbalized love for Ilse, and finally memory, the things one can never have. Woody Allen recognized the unspoken layers and texturing of the film and used them to inform his homage, PLAY IT AGAIN, SAM (1972).

Theme

The theme, or multiple themes, in a film *emerge as a function of the interplay among all the narrative and visual elements.* For example, in many westerns, the plot develops a conflict between opposing forces: sheepherders against farmers; marshall against bankrobber(s); cowboys against Indians. Or it may develop around the revenge of one brother against the other, as in WINCHESTER '73 (1950), or around the capture and imprisonment of a stagecoach robber, as in THE 3:10 TO YUMA (1957), but the *primary* **theme** of the film, the *main subject*, in all these cases, *is the struggle between good and evil.*

Theme, in literature and in film, *depends on understanding literal meanings and recognizing connotations*, often specifically, the *symbolic* dimensions of *textual connotation*. In THE 3:10 TO YUMA, a farmer, Dan Evans (Van Heflin), about to lose his land because of a severe drought, accepts the dangerous job of guarding an outlaw, Ben Wade (Glenn Ford), and putting him on the train (of the title) to the prison in Yuma. Evans takes on the job only because he wants to use the money offered to pay for water. While he and Wade wait for several hours, the outlaw tempts the farmer with promises of thousands of dollars if Evans allows him to to escape. Evans visibly struggles with temptation and the conflict becomes nearly Biblical, a struggle between Satan and a "good" man over possession of his soul.

By including the drought as an element in the narrative, a second theme is introduced—the struggle between life and death; neither the land nor the people can live without water. **The interaction among all the facets of the plot development**—*character, narrative, language, visual images*, **produces the themes**—*life and death, good against evil*. These themes enlarge the meaning of the film.

Symbol

A symbol *is anything that represents another thing; often a concrete object that stands for an abstract idea.* For example, the dove is a *symbol* of peace. Everything that *creates meaning* has a symbolic level; this is something of an oversimplification but will do for our present purposes. Symbols also have a literal and a connotative level and a cultural and textual dimension. *Cultural symbols* are those objects, ideas, notions that exist as an essential part of cultural knowledge. All cultures are associated with objects that take on specific symbolic meanings—from the national flag that represents the country to emblems with narrower significations: the Eiffel Tower represents Paris while the Empire State Building represents New York City and the Golden Gate Bridge represents San Francisco. The caricature of "Uncle Sam" stands for the United States; "John Bull" stands for England. These are the simplest of cultural symbols; most are more complex.

Symbols are not universal; they do not mean the same thing to people of all cultures. For example, in the United States the elephant stands for the Republican party but it is a religious symbol to the Hindus. Indeed, the symbols of one culture may not even be understood by another: the image of "fire in a lake," according to Chinese philosophy means "revolution and change," but few Westerners will know that. The meaning of the symbol depends on the definition the culture gives to it. Needless to say, a lack of knowledge will prevent recognition of cultural symbols other than our own; on the other hand, our own symbols are often so familiar that we think of their meanings as "natural" while their deeper implications often remain invisible.

Textual symbols, like textual connotation, emerge from the images and soundtrack of the film itself, that is, from the specific film "text" (see fig. 64). Objects and sounds may symbolize a character within the story: a man may be recognized by his battered hat or by the distinct melody he whistles. Or an object may symbolize a more abstract idea that contributes to the theme. Some symbols are indicated by a close-up or music or dialogue that directs the audience's attention to them. In the concluding sequence of CITIZEN KANE, the jigsaw puzzle is marked by

Figure 64. The Seventh Seal. Bergman's deliberate use of light and dark for symbolic purposes has already been noted (fig. 23). The symbolism of the shot goes even further. The chess game is a symbol of the knight's life. He might "put Death in check" this time but ultimately he must lose the game. As the film progresses Death takes the characters one by one, much as a chessplayer captures and removes his opponent's pieces.

the dialogue, by the lighting, and by the camera. A crane shot produces an overview of the warehouse crowded with crates, statues, paintings, all the objects Kane had collected during his lifetime. The scene looks like the jumble of a jigsaw before it is sorted; the point is made: the puzzle is the film's symbol of Charles Foster Kane's life.

By the end of THE 3:10 TO YUMA, the drought, a natural phenomenon, becomes a classical symbol of barrenness, a punishment of the inhabitants for their apathy and for allowing evil to spread through the land. As Evans struggles with his conscience and finally conquers his temptation to dishonesty, clouds gather and lighting strikes. Finally, when he has put the criminal on the train and so has contained the evil, it begins to rain, the *symbol* of purification and redemption, and the return of life-giving forces.

The Emperor's eyeglasses in Bernardo Bertolucci's film THE LAST EMPEROR (1987), provides another example. The discovery that the Emperor, Pu Yi, is near-sighted, the resistance of the temple guardians, and the introduction of a western doctor who can fit him for glasses are separate narrative occurrences, but concrete parts of the action. It later becomes clear that a symbolic connection exists between the threat of Pu Yi's blindness and the guardians' desire to keep him "blind" to what is going on inside and outside the walls of the Forbidden City because they fear the loss of their power.

As these examples illustrate, a full understanding of a symbol's significance is necessarily delayed until all the elements are presented through repeated appearances or references.

Motif

A motif *is the main theme or subject developed and elaborated in a work of art.* Visual motifs are also created through repetition. Motifs may be objects, visual or graphic patterns, narrative situations, phrases of dialogue that recur; often they are also symbols. In THE LAST EMPEROR bicycles become a motif through repeated references. First the Emperor's English tutor rides a bicycle in the palace. In those days, before the First World War, it was even in the Western world still a toy of the upper classes. Later, the young emperor, Pu Yi insists upon owning a bicycle, learns to ride, and even attempts to escape the palace on it. At the conclusion of the film, after Pu Yi has been "integrated" into Communist society, bicycles are visible by the hundreds in the background. The bicycle, once a symbol of the West, the upper classes, and progress, has become simply a mode of transportation for the masses, integrated, like Pu-Yi, himself, into modern Communist China.

As the object or element reappears, the motif develops and gains meaning. In WINCHESTER '73, the opening shot is a close-up of a perfect specimen of the famous rifle which is to be the prize in a shooting competition. The gun is won by Lynn McAdam (James Stewart) but it is stolen from him by his rival, "Dutch Henry" Brown. Subsequently the Winchester is the object of several thefts—by an Indian chief, an Army private, another hoodlum—until it is finally regained by its rightful owner. The rifle takes on increasing significance as an instrument that provokes unchecked desire and breeds violence and death.

Allusion

An allusion *is a mention or indirect reference to something external to the work in which it appears.* It may be a reference to another film, to a piece of writing, or to a current event. Allusions are very common in films, regularly used to extend the level of meaning beyond the visual presentation of the story. They can be brief asides, tributes to earlier films and filmmakers, cultural references as well. In their own films, Woody Allen and Brian DePalma make *allusion* to Eisenstein's *Odessa Steps* sequence. By including visual and verbal references to many filmmakers and writers who influenced him, Jean-Luc Godard pays homage to them.

An allusion may be a serious political and social comment. Some consider that RAMBO (1982) makes critical allusions to America's failure to deal properly with Vietnam veterans; MISSING (1982) alludes to American covert collaboration in the military overthrow of the Chilean government in 1973. THE MANCHURIAN CANDIDATE alludes to the tactics of 1950's "Red Scare" politicians.

Allusion is also a vital element in comic films. In NINE TO FIVE (1980), the revenge fantasies of the three protagonists, Dolly Parton, Lily Tomlin, and Jane Fonda, allude to previous styles of films while depicting the frustrating and oppressive working conditions of secretaries. In the movie AIRPLANE! (1980) the protagonist remembers his first encounter with the woman he loves; in his fantasy he dances with a bravado that alludes to the exaggerated dance style and posture made famous by John Travolta in SATURDAY NIGHT FEVER (1977). All take-offs, parodies, spoofs, and remakes, although they provide entertainment in their own right, depend for full understanding on the viewer's knowledge of the previous film, the basis of the satire. YOUNG FRANKENSTEIN

Figure 65. Young Frankenstein (d. Mel Brooks, 1974). The sets of the original 1931 FRANKENSTEIN were found and re-used for this spoof that depends on allusion to and recognition of the original for most of its humor.

(1974), SPACEBALLS (1987), PLAY IT AGAIN, SAM (1972), DEAD MEN DON'T WEAR PLAID (1982), PENNIES FROM HEAVEN (1981), THE PURPLE ROSE OF CAIRO (1985), and many, many others, all use "allusion" as the point of departure of their films.

In general, just as with connotation, symbols, motifs, and allusions, may also be understood on a "cultural" level (based on knowledge shared by a particular group) or on a "textual" level (based on the particular work itself). For example, the circle is a figure that stands for certain ideas in western culture: unity, cycles, endlessness, continuation. These meanings have grown out of the use artists, writers, and philosophers have made of the image of the circle; that is the cultural level. We shall see that in LITTLE BIG MAN, the image of the circle contains all of these established cultural meanings and adds other meaning specific to the film; that is the textual level.

Film Analysis

Arthur Penn's LITTLE BIG MAN, made in 1970, is a useful film to examine for an analysis of meaning. The film is a western but it is also a parody of the genre. It combines many of the standard mythical elements of the western with sharp criticism and political allusion. Using all the elements defined in this section—signs, symbols, motifs, allusion—the film brings together levels of both cultural and textual connotation which finally, evoke larger themes, of harmony and balance, tolerance and moderation. Produced during the political and social turmoil of the Vietnam War era the film sharply criticizes American military aggression, attitudes toward war, and in general, American morality and values.

LITTLE BIG MAN is the story of Jack Crabbe (Dustin Hoffman), a white man, raised by the Cheyenne Indians and, as he says, "the sole white survivor of the Battle of the Little Bighorn, popularly known as Custer's Last Stand." Through a series of adventures, he moves back and forth between Indian and white societies, and, having lived in both, is able to compare, contrast, and evaluate each of them. The two sharply contrasting ways of life are presented "through his eyes." Cinematic devices are used to control the way the information is presented. The filmmakers' position on the issues is never in question; their preference and respect is defined in every point from the framing and composition of each frame to the narrative line.

The film begins in the "present," 1970, with a close-up of the now very old Jack Crabbe talking into a historian's tape recorder. As he tells his story, which began one hundred and eleven years before and covers about ten years, a dissolve moves the scene to the open prairie where a wagon train lies in ruins. His narration becomes a voice-over as he relates the facts of his life: rescued from the Pawnee raid by the Cheyenne, until his late teens he lived with them and learned their language, hunting skills, and their philosophy of life and moral order. The tribe named him "Little Big Man" because, although he was small in size, he had displayed great courage when he saved another brave from a Pawnee attack.

During a battle between the Cheyenne and the U.S. Cavalry, Little Big Man is captured and sent to live with Mr. and Mrs. Pendrake, a Baptist minister and his wife. From them Jack receives a white man's education and Christian moral training; he leaves them abruptly after discovering the minister's wife (whom he admires) making love to a shopkeeper.

Jack tries various occupations on the frontier but fails at all of them and eventually moves West. On the way, his stagecoach is attacked by Indians and his Swedish wife, Olga, is kidnapped. While searching for her in Indian territory, Jack is captured by his former brothers and returns for a time to his tribe. Then, in order to continue his search for Olga, he leaves them and attaches himself to Custer's regiment. After seeing the army slaughter an entire encampment of Indian women and children he deserts and returns once again to the Cheyenne. A happy year with an Indian wife follows but ends when, during another massacre—this one led and encouraged by General Custer —he watches as his wife and newly-born child are killed.

At this point Jack wants badly to assassinate Custer but fails to carry out his plan and, ashamed of his weakness, he becomes first a drunkard among the whites and then a hermit. On the verge of suicide, he catches sight of Custer's regiment on the move, and decides he must finally "face the devil and send him back to Hell." He rejoins the regiment as a scout; when Custer asks his opinion on whether to attack the Indians at the Little Bighorn or retreat, Jack, knowing the odds against him, tells him to attack. In the famous battle, Custer and his entire regiment are, of course, wiped out. Jack, however, is saved by an Indian and is returned to what remains of his Cheyenne family and to Old Lodgeskins, his adopted grandfather and teacher (played by Chief Dan George).

The old man, decides he is ready to die and reminds his adopted son of the beliefs held by the Cheyenne for whom "everything is alive" in contrast to those of the white man for whom, he says, everything is dead, and he foretells the end of the Cheyenne. The film ends with the Chief's stoical and good-humored recognition of the inevitable ironies of life.

Jack is unable to accept the values guiding white civilization—hypocrisy, greed, lust for power and money. He is equally unable to accept the Cheyenne's fate at the hands of the white man and so must remain an outsider to both cultures. The film is tightly structured around this opposition between the two ways of life. Among the whites, life is linear, goal-oriented, and exploitive; Jack moves through "periods" in his life. Whatever he does, he is always searching for an identity, trying to fit into society's mold, *becoming* something else. When his "religious" period ends in revelations of hypocrisy, he enters his "snake-oil salesman" period but he is too honest. Reunited with his sister Caroline, he learns from her how to shoot and enters his "gunfighter" period but he is sickened when Wild Bill Hickock shoots a man in cold blood. Unable to kill for the sake of a reputation, he becomes a storekeeper but he does not understand that his partner is a cheat and he loses everything. In every case, he learns that he must take advantage of others.

Figure 66. Little Big Man (d. Arthur Penn, 1970). An eye-level shot but from down low. Jack Crabbe in white society, in the gutter (See fig. 67).

In contrast, the Indians's way of life emphasizes harmony, *being* over *becoming*. Individuals grow older, some are killed in encounters with the white man, new families are formed, and the tribe moves across the plains, but their way of life and beliefs include and tolerate their fellows. They live according to the naturally changing cycles of seasons. They question the senseless cruelty they experience and suffer and yet, free of anger, taking the long view, they accept their fate. Among the Cheyenne, all feelings are expressed directly and a variety of life-styles is tolerated; in white society people say one thing and do another. Mrs. Pendrake, the minister's wife, pretends to be pure, a God-fearing, respectable woman but behaves sinfully. General Custer seems, at a distance, to be great and noble but up close he emerges as a megalomaniacal, tyrannical, arrogant madman. Mr. Pendrake pretends to be a man of God, yet relishes the thought of beating religion into young Jack.

The abstract **theme** of the importance of appearances in white civilization is underlined by a visual motif that makes it concrete: *mirrors*. Characters repeatedly examine themselves in mirrors as though checking to see that they fit the part they have chosen to play. Mrs. Pendrake's lover is holding a small mirror in his hand as he smoothes his mustache and in which he sees her when she walks into his store. Mr. Merriweather, the "flim-flam" man, primps in front of a little mirror outside of his tent just before he and Jack are tarred and feathered. Jack sees the reflection of Wild Bill Hickock in a barroom mirror before he sees the man, a fitting introduction to a myth. And Custer, seated before a mirror, calmly trims his mustache, after Jack fails to kill him. After discovering Mrs. Pendrake with her lover, Jack, too, now a part of that society, studies himself in a mirror as though to register the deep change in him that the experience has caused. Vanity is everywhere; appearance is more important than substance, a mere reflection of reality.

Life among the Indians seems to be straightforward and direct, not two-faced as it is among the whites. The Indians are generous, accepting, and forgiving. They have no pretensions about sexuality, have no interest in domination, and make no issue of wealth. They see a center to life, a moral and spiritual essence around which all things circle and which gives meaning and balance to existence. Chief Old Lodgeskins' statement that the whites do not know where the center of the earth is becomes another aspect of the Indian moral vision of the "circle of life." Time, seasons, day, cycles—meaning is embraced in the circle of life.

The *symbol* of the circle was introduced at an earlier point in the film, as an element essential to Indian life at even the most basic level: the teepee is circular in shape; the Indian camp is roughly circular in its arrangement. Later, Little Big Man convinces his grandfather to escape by persuading him that they must flee to the river which "is part of the great circle of the waters of the earth." The orderly, cyclical nature of the Indians' ways is visually contrasted to that of the whites whose activity is either linear—regiments of marching soldiers—or chaotic, the massacres.

The circle in the Indians' moral and spiritual vision of life becomes a key *motif* of the movie. It is developed both visually and in the dialogue. Through the motif, the filmmakers criticize the values and obsessions of the American establishment one hundred years after the setting of the story.

While the Indians are shown as innocent victims, the whites are shown as swindlers, cheats, and killers, desperate for financial success, succumbing to restless dissatisfaction with limits, and experiencing only moral bankruptcy. The moral emptiness of white American society is a primary *theme* of LITTLE BIG MAN and is developed through another motif—the massacre. Through the repetition of the attacks by the United States military on the Indian women and children, director, Arthur Penn and the producer, Stuart Millar set out to expose the myth of the westward expansion and to present the hidden side of the historical record, including the systematic murder and brutal resettlement of native Americans. By 1970 the Civil Rights movement had raised American consciousness about the treatment and attitudes towards blacks and, by extension, towards all racial groups. The film makes no compromises on this point.

Several aspects of the film show that it is not just a "period piece" about Custer's Last Stand, but relates directly to the controversy over American military intervention in Vietnam that ripped the United States in the late sixties. Many Americans at that time were preoccupied with questions about the reasons for being in Vietnam, the right to be there at all, and about atrocities being committed against the Vietnamese civilian population in the name of anti-Communism. Some critics saw LITTLE BIG MAN as a denunciation of American policy in Southeast Asia and while the film did not precisely re-enact events that occurred in Vietnam, as did Ralph Nelson's SOLDIER BLUE (made the same year and reportedly directly influenced by the massacre at My Lai), the attacks on the women and children in LITTLE BIG MAN cannot fail to recall that criminal incident. The drive of the whites in the film, for money and power mingles with a racism that, for them, justifies the genocide of the Indians. When Custer says with nearly hysterical hate and contempt that the Indian women "breed like rats," he clearly means (and is understood to mean) that they must be exterminated like rats. His personal hatred hides the coincidental results of the genocide—the appropriation of the land. Again, the criticisms are clearly stated and the viewer is convinced to condemn him.

Outspoken as the filmmakers were on the issues of racism and military aggression, they revealed themselves to be considerably less progressive in their treatment of women. It is well-known that the roles for women in film are usually stereotypical, with their real concerns and plight either mocked or ignored. LITTLE BIG MAN is no exception. While Jack Crabbe and his grandfather, Old Lodgeskins are clearly the only fully developed characters in the film, the male secondary characters emerge as individuals—Custer's vanity and egotism are as neatly drawn as his racism; Merriweather is so careless with himself in his drive for success that each time he appears, he is missing another hand or a leg or an eye. Among the Cheyenne, Shadow-Who-Comes-Inside and Younger Bear are individuals, each with his own personality and qualities.

The women characters have no role but that of stereotypical foils. Jack's older sister, Caroline, "wants" to be raped by the Indians and, as a result of their "rejection," turns into a man-hater. "Miz" Pendrake (Faye Dunaway who had played Bonnie in Penn's BONNIE AND CLYDE [1967] was featured) is sketched as a sexually avid woman, the unfaithful wife of a strait-laced preacher, seductive, and lusting after Jack, her adopted son. She is last seen, having fallen on bad days, as a prostitute. Olga is sketched as the typical middle-class white woman who, once she is stolen by the Indians, becomes the "boss" of the family—a shrew. The Cheyenne women, Sunshine and her sisters, are so-called "natural" women, subservient and passive women free of puritanical hang-ups about monogamy and fidelity. The Indians as a group represent the sixties counter-culture; the women in particular represent the fantasy of "free love" carried by Sunshine's insistence on sharing Little Big Man with her "sisters." Women's issues and treatment are neglected here as elsewhere in the Hollywood feature, the dominant form of narrative film.

Sequence Analysis

How are these abstract meanings conveyed? Let us examine in detail a single sequence that contributes directly to the creation of the motifs and imagery of the film. The sequence occurs early in the film, immediately after the young Jack Crabbe has become a warrior and has earned the name "Little Big Man." At the end of the naming ceremony, a cut moves the scene to the small band moving across the plains. The scouts suddenly catch sight of smoke on the horizon and they ride off to investigate.

Literal Meaning: The braves ride into the middle of an Indian encampment that has been burned and is still smoldering. The covering has burned off and only the frames of teepees remain. The bodies of the Indian inhabitants and debris are scattered everywhere. The camera holds on the bodies of several children and women. In a medium shot, Little Big Man/Jack says to Old Lodgeskins, "I don't understand it, Grandfather. Why would they kill women and children?" The old man replies, "Because they are strange. . . ." The camera, tracking, pauses on a saddlebag with the words "U.S. Army" stenciled on it, lying on the ground. He continues, "they do not seem to know where the center of the earth is." The camera cuts from one shot to another of the dead Indians. The next shot shows one of the Cheyenne braves who has returned from an investigation of the whole area. In sign language he reports that everyone is dead. The old man says: "We must have a war on these cowards and teach them a lesson." Cut to the next sequence as the Cheyenne prepare for battle with the Cavalry.

Cultural connotation: Americans have been taught two contradictory myths about Indians. One, deriving from the Puritan fear of the wilderness and its inhabitants, saw the Indians as bloodthirsty, uncivilized, savages who lacked moral decency and respect for the property of others. The other myth, arising from 17th Century European idealizations of the New World, saw the Indians as "noble savages," at one with nature and free of the corruption of civilization.

These contrasting ideas about Indians are part of American culture, and allow most viewers to accept movies in which scantily dressed men with feathers in their hair ride wildly out of ravines, ready to kill, brandishing spears and shrieking at the top of their lungs. Viewers can also accept a calm, wise elder, a weathered Indian Chief, in full feathered head-dress, speaking words of wisdom about life and nature in poetic phrases.

Early in America's history, the notion of the wilderness as a spiritual place, free from the corruptions of society developed. The Indian, the original inhabitant of the wilderness, theoretically had more access to this spiritual side of nature but until the '60's Hollywood preferred to use the image of the bloodthirsty savage. Although the figure of the "noble savage" (see fig. 68) appeared from time to time in the western genre (most notably in John Ford's CHEYENNE AUTUMN, made in 1964) LITTLE BIG MAN develops the individual in detail, casting an Indian as the Chief and in the lesser native American roles, concentrating on the culture of the Cheyenne, however romanticized it may be.

Figure 67. Little Big Man. Chief Old Lodgeskins and Little Big Man at the place of the first massacre. "But grandfather, why would they kill woman and children?" "Because they are strange." The low angle sets them off against the sky giving them both heroic stature. The two societies are opposed, as the sky is opposed to the mud (see fig. 66).

In the sequence under examination, the myths are presented indirectly, through characters, setting, and circumstances. Instead of being told, we are shown. Let us look first at the setting. In the transitional shots that

154

Figure 68. Little Big Man. The "Noble Indian."

lead into the sequence under examination, the Cheyenne are travelling across the plains. In the foreground, buffalo graze placidly, undisturbed by the presence of the Indians. The shot suggests that Indian and buffalo share the land and are part of a harmonious balance of nature. A later scene of buffalo hunters stacking huge piles of skins contrasts with the peaceful balance of the Indians and underlines the rapacious nature of the whites.

The first shot of the sequence shows the Indians, quite small in a wide expanse of yellow grassland, as they ride off to investigate the smoke they have seen. The open spaces offer little protection and, along with the smallness of the group in the wide land, that suggests their vulnerability, their supreme self-confidence, and also their courage in the face of possible danger. These perceptions are reinforced by the next shot of the burned out Indian village followed by a closer look at the destruction of this Indian camp. The camera holds on the image of dead women and children in the encampment which is a powerful image in view of the social moral and cultural taboo against the murder of women and children even in war. The controversies that raged over American activities in Southeast Asia make these images a strong reference to what became an issue of killing and maiming women and children. The fire is smoldering;

only tent frames and tattered, smoking remnants remain, *suggesting* that the immediate danger is past but also that there has been a massacre: bodies of men, women and children are sprawled randomly, clearly caught unawares, in the middle of their daily routine, not the result of a battle between equal forces.

Old Lodgeskins, already established as wise and moral, comments on the scene. His troubled, thoughtful expression, his stylized and lyrical, poetic speech contribute to the image of the wise and moral man—in short, he is the personification of the "noble Indian." It must be pointed out that the representation of the Indians is not completely accurate and factual. The portrayal of the Cheyenne is an idealized one, as much of a myth as the heroic cowboy or gunfighter. Penn uses these mythic qualities thematically. The Indians' harmony with nature, their integrity, tolerance, and simplicity make them representative of the sixties' counter-culture, which embraced these same values. The contrast between the harmony among the Cheyenne and the atrocities witnessed by them in this sequence introduces the theme of an intolerant and brutal white society, out of balance with nature.

These cultural connotations are developed in the **textual connotation**, arising out of the text. The close shot of the burned Indian village in this sequence introduces the textual symbol of the circle which continues to develop through other references. The point is that the soldiers, "who do not know where the center of the earth is," have destroyed the teepees. While the circular aspect of the destruction is less important than the fact of the destruction itself, it adds to the larger moral contrast between the whites and the Indians.

What is the point of the emphasis on the bodies in the village? Wouldn't wider shots of the scene have made clear what had taken place? Yes. But *massacre* becomes a recurring motif and develops as a key element in the film and does not depend entirely on simple presentation of the facts. The emotional impact is created by the subtle differences and variations among the several incidents. In this first case, the scene is the aftermath, calm, still, quiet; it is all over. The viewer can tolerate the scene. The subsequent scenes become increasingly difficult to stand as the viewer is forced closer and closer to the murders.

The textual connotations originate in the pre-title sequence of the film when the historian, interviewing the ancient Jack Crabbe, says, with an embarrassed laugh, that the American treatment of the Indians bordered on genocide. This statement represents the political position of the film. Later, the methodical murder of the helpless women and children under Custer's orders cannot help but remind the audience of the parallels between the genocide of native Americans, and that of the Holocaust and also of the Vietnamese.

Penn develops the massacre into a motif by showing separate attacks on the Cheyenne by the United States Cavalry. The first one has preceded this sequence and only "names" the culprits through the tracking shot over the dead bodies and the U.S. Army saddlebag. The second one moves the camera (and thereby the viewer) closer to the victims; and in the third one, at the Wachita River, the camera, the protagonist, the victims, and the viewer are all together in the very midst of the horror surrounded by cries, pain, chaos and endless death (see fig. 69). Little Big Man (and the viewer with him) watches helplessly as his Cheyenne wife, Sunshine, carrying their baby and running in desperation, is shot over and over by a soldier.

The textual connotation of the whole sequence is unified around the figure of Old Lodgeskins and his words. The camera shows him in a

Figure 69. Little Big Man. The massacre at the Wachita River. Sunshine flees toward the camera and Little Big Man (and the audience); the cavalry officer shoots her. In the sequence, the audience's view is associated and allied with that of Little Big Man.

close-up against the sky, his wise, sad gaze and Little Big Man's shocked one counterpointed with the scene of the slaughter. By the way the camera frames him, and by the weight and tone of his speech, we are led to understand that Old Lodgeskins is a man to be listened to and trusted. He becomes the spokesman for the film's **moral theme**: the whites lack respect for life; the "human beings" (as the Cheyenne refer to themselves) know where the "center of the earth" is and have a profound moral vision of life.

Conclusion

While this analysis is by no means exhaustive, it is clear that the **theme** of the film as a whole is present even in this one brief sequence. The first specific presentation of the issue of American military aggression, the first formal contrast of Indian moral vision and white moral corruption are introduced. The contrast is made by the juxtaposition of the old man's words with the image of the army saddlebag. "They," the soldiers of the U.S. Army, are responsible for this atrocity and "they" have no morality. The political position of the film is clearly critical of the soldiers—and by extension, white society. In this chapter we have briefly discussed the narrative film LITTLE BIG MAN in order to illustrate how a film makes meaning and how that meaning affects the viewer.

CHAPTER 8
Production, Distribution, Exhibition

Americans see an overwhelming number of American films; well over ninety percent of the films exhibited and available to viewers in the US today are produced in this country. The foreign industries some of which, like India's, are larger than that of the United States have no distribution outlets here and therefore their products are rarely seen. In the United States, even with the competition of television, the movie business is still a large industry—producing over four hundred films and grossing about 4 billion dollars a year—and like any other industry its object is to "maximize profits," so box office receipts are much more important to the senior executives than "art," "social conscience," or "education," aspects that concern anyone interested in studying the medium.

Throughout this book, we have been examining film as a means of expression, integrating technical and artistic issues, looking at the elements that enable it to tell stories, create emotions, convey ideas and information. Our concern has been with the way movies make meaning (process) and how to "read" that meaning (interpretation). Of course, we can learn to "read" a film without understanding the business side of filmmaking and in fact, most people do not think very much about that "other side" of the movies, but without knowing something of the behind-the-scenes activity that produces the finished films—financing, distribution, and exhibition—an important element to complete understanding is missing because, in the end, that side determines *what* we see and how we see it. Decisions made by various executives—of studios, distributors, television stations, video cassette companies—affect the kinds and number of films made, and therefore, what we see.

A Historical Note

It is hard to conceive of the economic and social power the movies had in their heyday, in the 1930's and '40's. At that time, the studios earned huge sums of money through world-wide film rentals and owned expensive real estate properties, largely in the form of theatres located in valuable urban areas across this country. The five largest studios then—Warner Brothers, Metro-Goldwyn-Mayer, Paramount, RKO, and Twentieth Century-Fox—controlled all aspects of the film process: they made the movies, operated distribution outlets that rented out the movies, and owned the chains of theatres which played them. This kind of structure was called *"vertical integration"* and meant nearly unlimited artistic and financial control by the studios over the film material.

With that much control over production, distribution, and exhibition, the "Big Five," as they were called, gained a virtual monopoly over the whole movie business. After all, the producers chose the screenplays and, since they kept directors, actors, and crews under long-term contract, they could put together a production without having to bargain over each film. The producers also planned the publicity campaigns, had them carried out, made sure the films were shown where and when they wished, and all at the prices they set. Control of the theatres was most important in eliminating competition because the studios could count in advance on having any and all of their films accepted for theatrical release.

The deal was that the exhibitors agreed, before the films were even made and knowing neither the titles nor the subject matter, to show an entire *block* of films produced by the studios. Called "block" or "blind booking," it later became the basis of a government anti-trust suit against the studios which argued that such practices fixed prices and restricted competitive bidding. But for the time being, between 1920 and 1940, the American film industry grew unchecked into a monopoly of enormous power. The First World War had devastated the foreign film industries, while Hollywood, untouched, continued to be fully productive. Europe was hungry for cheap entertainment and American films were readily available. The market and the product were in perfect harmony.

In spite of the Depression and throughout the thirties the movie industry remained healthy and powerful within the larger entertainment industry. In fact, by the forties it had grown so successful that it was considered "Depression-proof." No one could imagine a time when this would no longer be true. But ironically, the Second World War, while it brought enormous wealth to the industry, was also followed by serious social, economic and political upheavals that threatened to destroy Hollywood and did, in fact, dismantle the old system. Four major factors are considered responsible for the change.

Four Factors of Change

• 1. The demographics of the American population changed. Most important, the post-war baby boom began in 1946 and gradually both disposable income and free time grew limited. It became less convenient and more expensive for families with babies to get out for an evening at the movies. Also the war-time shortages of gasoline and goods were over and people were spending money on homes, especially in the suburbs, on appliances, on cars, on vacations, and on their children. Other kinds of entertainment—theatre, music, nightclubs—that had been unavailable during the war were once again attracting consumers. Suddenly the movies which had been the only form of escape was only one of many. The number of movie theatre admissions fell sharply.

• 2. Coinciding with the post-war return to the home and family, TV arrived on the scene. In 1947 there were only 14,000 TV sets in America, fewer than one in eight homes, but in 1950, only three years later there were 4 million, and four years after that, in 1954, 32 million. Those are increases of several hundreds of percents in just a few short years. In 1962, less than 15 years after the introduction of television, it was estimated that ninety percent of all American homes had a set and people of all ages were spending many hours a week in front of it. (Today it is estimated that the TV is "on" 7.5 hours per day and that "saturation" has been reached, with about 98 percent of households, owning multiple TV sets. More homes have TV sets than have indoor plumbing!).

During the early fifties, and as a direct result of the proliferation of TV, attendance at movie theatres fell by twenty-five percent. TV was stealing the very same audience that had gone faithfully twice a week to the movies for escapist entertainment and had paid to see melodramas, family shows, comedies, thrillers, horror and sci-fi movies, and of course, westerns. TV programming was based on these genres, plus old movies . . . all "for free." During that period, about one quarter of all movie theatres, 4000 out of approximately 18,000, closed (although, interestingly, the other great post-war commercial phenomenon, the automobile, contributed to a replacement—the drive-in theatre which became very popular, at least seasonally).

• 3. Another factor that affected Hollywood was the anti-trust suit the government brought against the studios in 1948. Known as the

"Paramount decrees" (it was the largest), the suit was not the first attack on the monopolistic practices of the industry, but it was the last and most successful effort at separating film production and distribution from ownership of the theatres.

Until that time, because of ownership of the theatres, the studios had been able to distribute their movies with no regard to quality and at prices they themselves set. Although it took many years after the 1948 Supreme Court decision for the studios to comply, by the late fifties they had sold off many of their theatres: out of the 1,395 theatres giant Paramount owned in 1945 only 534 remained in 1957, while the relatively small RKO had owned 109 theatres in 1945 but only 82 in 1957.

The divestiture immediately increased competition from both American independent filmmakers and foreign studios because rental fees had suddenly become competitive and they were able to place their films. The judgement against the studios was hard on Hollywood, coming at a time the industry was already vulnerable due to a failing market, the result of all the other factors.

• 4. The last factor was political and involved ethical and human issues: the blacklist. The blacklist was a list of people, accused by their colleagues of being Communists and who, as a result, were deprived of their jobs. How did the blacklist come into being?

The origins of the situation go back to the 1930's and a legislative committee that was established to investigate Communist activities in the United States. During World War II, the committee's investigations were curtailed because the United States was temporarily allied with the Soviet Union against Nazism. Once the war was over, the Cold War began and Russia, once again, became the enemy; McCarthyism began to rise; and the House of Representatives' Committee on Un-American Activities was reborn.

Beginning in 1947, and continuing well into the '50's, the House Committee, "HUAC," as it was called, held hearings on so-called Communist infiltration of Hollywood and, because it was Hollywood, those hearings attracted a great deal of media attention. Although the Committee called many film industry people to testify about their past political affiliations, they particularly sought out Hollywood stars. After all, the stars were famous and for a Committee member to be photographed with the likes of John Wayne, Humphrey Bogart, or Judy Holliday, meant enormous publicity.

In those days, the movies were as much a part of daily life as TV is today; movie magazines and Hollywood gossip columnists were popular and powerful, writing about the stars for a public hungry for juicy details about them. If Hedda Hopper or Louella Parsons, the two most famous columnists, *happened* to mention the name of a Representative who *happened* to be questioning a famous actor, it could only help the politician's career. Respectable newspapers saw a respectable way to cash in on the market for gossip and the legislators cashed in on the stars' publicity.

Looking back we can see that the hearings were divisive and damaging not only to those individuals who were fired from their jobs, but to the whole film community. People were called as witnesses and asked to name friends and acquaintances they knew to be members of the Communist Party (which, it should be noted, was never illegal in the United States); they found themselves confronted with an ethical decision. Some few powerful individuals, like Lillian Hellman and Humphrey Bogart, refused. Some pleaded with the Committee to excuse them and save them from becoming "stool-pigeons." Others took the first or the fifth amendment and then found themselves blacklisted because they had been "unfriendly" witnesses or simply because "taking the 5th" came to imply guilt. Others named names. The "friendly" witnesses gave the names of people they accused often without proof, of being Communists or "fellow travellers" (Communist sympathizers). Without a trial, without the opportunity of answering or disproving the charges, those named were immediately barred from working in Hollywood.

We now know that from 1950 to 1960, a blacklist existed of between 200 and 300 people (although the fear was so great that much higher figures were imagined) who were not permitted to work in the Hollywood film industry. In 1960, Universal Pictures decided to release the film SPARTACUS and to give screen credit openly to its writer, Dalton Trumbo. Trumbo, one of the "Hollywood Ten," had been jailed for contempt of Congress, released, blacklisted, and for years had been writing under an assumed name. With Universal's action the blacklist began its slow collapse.

The Legacy of the Blacklist

How did the blacklist hurt Hollywood? For one thing, some very talented individuals who were denied work left the industry and took their skills and creative ideas with them. For another, the film community broke into two groups and, depending on their political views, they saw the accusers as informers or patriots and the accused as either victims or traitors. That ideological split in the close-knit movies industry generated rage and bitterness.

Then too, the idea that jobs could be lost because of a rumor or gossip, caused such general fear and insecurity that a shift occurred in the kinds of movies that the industry dared to make. Writers were afraid to write; producers were afraid to produce; directors were afraid of being associated with a politically questionable film. Innovation or any new ideas, which might have benefited Hollywood in its battle against television, could not be risked. Subject matter and form could not be innovative because if the resulting film was too difficult, it might be misunderstood, seen as "subversive," or leftist or just dangerously different.

Dealing with these factors was very difficult for Hollywood which, until the fifties, had not needed to be the least bit flexible and had never needed to consider such problems. In any case, the industry could do little about the baby boom except wait for the kids to grow up and become movie-goers themselves; all it did about the blacklist was wait until the American political climate gradually changed and HUAC lost its power. What it *chose* to do about TV and the Paramount decrees permanently affected the industry.

Hollywood vs. Television

In retrospect, and with more than 40 years of clear-eyed hindsight, Hollywood's response to TV seems fairly predictable: do what TV cannot do. If the TV screen is small, make the movie screen enormous; if the TV is in black and white, make the movies "in living color" and go for colorful stories and locations; if TV flattens the image, give movies the illusion of three dimensions; if TV only shows family fare, offer more risky adult subjects and go after the youth audience. So when, in 1953, the box office success of Cinerama (a travelogue but in a complicated 3-D process) seemed to prove that people would go out to see something they could not see at home, Hollywood regained hope. It thought it had a key to success.

The industry continued to perfect its mixture of tame, diluted subject matter (love stories, comedies, adventures), and simple forms (musicals, historical costume dramas, extravaganzas), but added new technology. First came 3-D with plastic glasses (Hitchcock made DIAL M FOR MURDER in 1954 using this process), and then wide-screen productions without glasses: CinemaScope, VistaVision and Todd A-O. Whenever the box office gross dipped, which it did rather unpredictably throughout the '50's, Hollywood, looking for the winning formula, would try something else: even larger musicals, horror films based on the effects of radioactivity, youth culture films, sexploitation films, "blacksploitation" films.

From time to time it looked as if the movies had made a successful stand against TV. But actually the silver screen could not hold out against the tiny tube; production costs were already so high that return on investment was not assured. The theaters suffered first and closed by the hundreds. Rather quickly, the production studios moved to collaborate with the new medium, recognizing that rather than competing, they could harvest a share of TV's many new markets. They began by selling old films to TV, then more recent ones, and very soon, big features; then they began to produce films specifically for TV and finally to produce the TV shows themselves. By the 1970's, the relationship between TV and film was flourishing and once again Hollywood was earning huge profits for the shareholders of the banks and conglomerates that had acquired the studios. In the last two decades, other changes, mostly in the expansion of screening outlets, have increased the demand for movies, and more flexible financial arrangements have increased the possibility of satisfying that demand.

Current Practice

The fact is that the television industry dwarfs the movie industry. Just to give an idea of the relative position of the two areas of entertainment, it has been noted that the international gross receipts from Paramount's greatest hit, RAIDERS OF THE LOST ARK (1981) were less than the syndication rights of "Cheers" and "All in the Family." The industry continues to gross about 4 billion dollars a year, producing around 450 films (412 in 1984, 452 in 1985, 475 in 1986, and approximately the same in 1987). The problem is that production costs have skyrocketed and, as a result, the return on the investment has become risky and relatively small.

"The bottom line" was as important to film industry executives during Hollywood's "Golden Age" as it is today and, as a result of that preoccupation with profit, most of the factors that were operative in the industry's old days continue today. The "players" have changed somewhat—the two-tier division between the "majors" and the independents has added another level, the so-called "mini-majors." Today, the two largest "majors" are Warners and Paramount, with Columbia and Twentieth Century close behind. These companies are all mutations of the old studios. The surprise is that the fifth major studio is now Disney, or

Buena Vista, as its distribution arm is called. United Artists, now owned by CNN's Ted Turner, barely holds its place among the majors. The mini-majors, each of which began as a distributor, are Orion, Tri-Star, and Cannon. The distinction between "major" and "mini-major" is based on the number of films each has in production at any one time and the budgets for them. Independent filmmakers put together their own financing to make the films which are then "picked up" and distributed by the studios, through their well-established outlets.

The basic process of filmmaking continues to involve three stages, production, distribution, exhibition. **The producer** *supervises the overall construction of the film*: s/he puts together what is nowadays called a "package," selecting the story or screenplay ("the property"), the actors, and the "right" director. The producer arranges financing, controls expenditures and oversees all the "business" details of the production. Once the film is finished, "in the can," **the distributor** *markets the film and arranges for exhibition in theatres or on TV.* These areas remain unchanged.

Production changed first, because of the increase in foreign competition and most recently because of the video cassette recorder. The film industries in Europe were just getting back on their feet after two wars within three decades. Largely subsidized by their governments, they had less need to make a huge profit. At the same time, long cultural and artistic traditions left them freer than the Americans to present frank social and sexual subject matter and to experiment with new cinematic forms. Because investment capital was not easily available, the European film industries had to keep their budgets low so the films had a break-even point lower than that of American companies. These companies quickly recognized that there was a great potential for profit in these foreign film industries because of lower production costs. And a fringe benefit was new and interesting locations.

American producers began to finance American films overseas (foreshadowing by about a decade the transfer of other industries to foreign locales). In the sixties, American companies simply began to invest outright in foreign productions and by the late sixties and early seventies, slightly less than half of the feature films made by American companies were produced abroad. During the seventies, more than half the revenue of American film companies came from showing their films in foreign countries. The relationship between the American film industry and those abroad is so great that in 1988 all 5 films competing for the

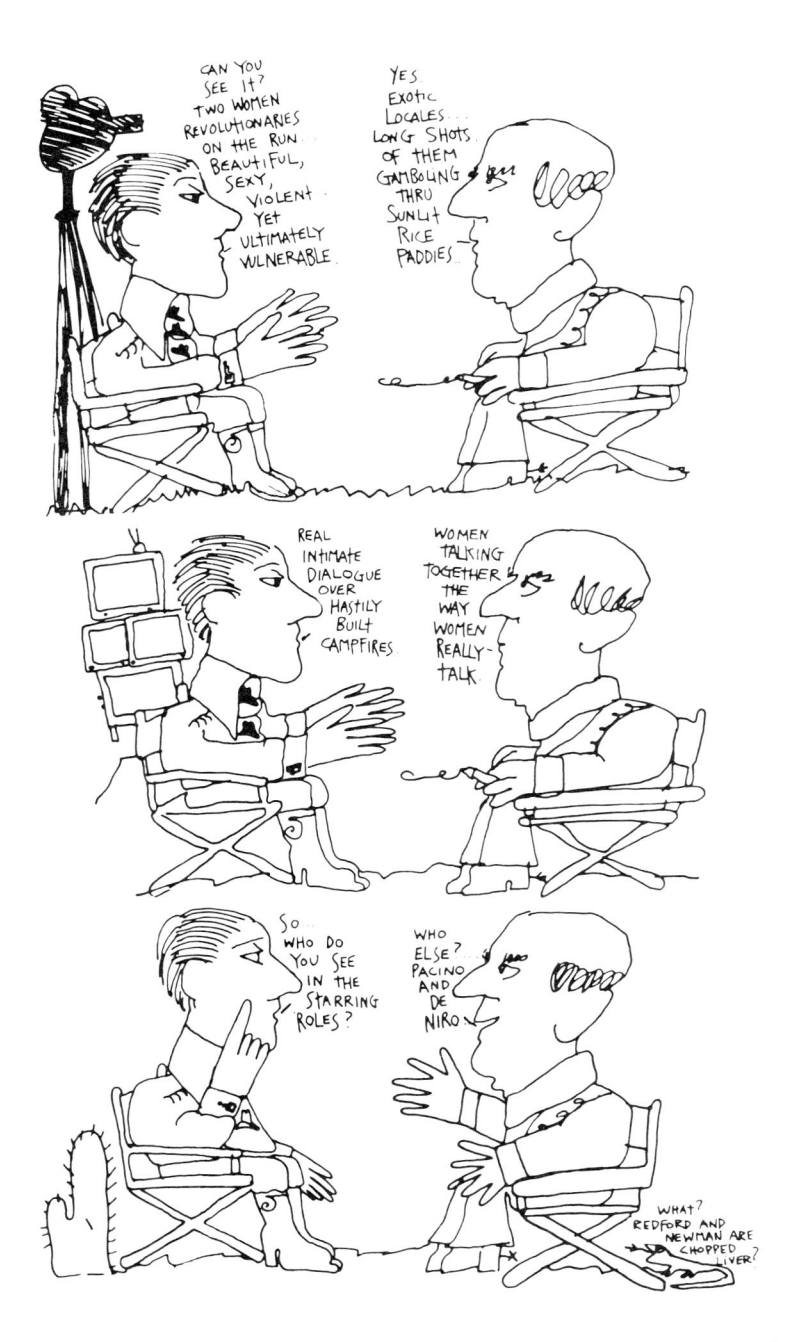

Figure 70. Cartoonist Nicole Hollander comments on the plight of women in movies. Hollywood producers control all areas of American studio production. From *I'm In Training to Be Tall and Blonde.* © Nicole Hollander, 1979. Reprinted by permission of the artist.

Academy Award, were directed by foreign directors, using American venture capital and studio facilities.

The other area that has changed significantly is exhibition. In the past, exhibition meant showing the movies in a theatre and the exhibitor was a theatre owner. By the end of the 1950's, TV had become another outlet and more recently Cable channels and videotape releases have become additional outlets. Coincidentally, distribution and exhibition have been taken over by the same corporations that own the studios, so in spite of the "Paramount Decrees" and divestiture, once again, "vertical integration" has become typical within the industry.

Production

Producers have retained a controlling position in the area of finance. Traditionally they have had control in all other areas: they may bring in writers to change the script, hire and fire directors. They can pressure directors to speed up production or bring down costs. They can even demand "the right of final cut." The producers in the current time resemble the old-time Hollywood producers. Woody Allen, produces his films independently but has enough of a "track record" and following to ensure distribution through the studios, retain virtually complete control over his material. Only directors who have their own production companies—George Lucas, Francis Coppola, Steven Spielberg—have control over their films. But for most directors, the alternative is independent production which has become significant. Out of the 475 films produced in 1986, less than half were made by the studios; the majority were independently produced.

A filmmaker who wants creative control must oversee the whole process: s/he plans the idea for the film, raises the money, rents equipment, hires the crew, shoots, and edits, and finally tries to interest one of the major studios in distributing the film. Some independent filmmakers have become well-known and relatively successful as *auteurs*. John Sayles, beginning in 1980, made a string of well-received films, including THE RETURN OF THE SECAUCUS 7, BROTHER FROM ANOTHER PLANET, LIANNA, BABY IT'S YOU, among others, and most recently, MATEWAN. Spike Lee began with a very low budget film, SHE'S GOTTA HAVE IT. Its success enabled him to make SCHOOL DAZE. Jim Jarmusch's history is quite similar: STRANGER THAN PARADISE received a great deal of attention from Vincent Canby, the *New York Times* film reviewer, which was enough to get it distributed nationally.

Robert Townsend produced HOLLYWOOD SHUFFLE, which was released directly onto videotape for distribution. Other independent productions such as EL NORTE (1983), THE TRIP TO BOUNTIFUL (1985) and BELIZAIRE, THE CAJUN (1986) were made as a result of workshops at Robert Redford's Sundance Institute. Geared to a popular audience, but quite a bit less commercial than the usual Hollywood film, these productions were true alternatives to Hollywood made on relatively low budgets and several received critical acclaim. With the increase in demand for films and the high cost of production, independent filmmakers will undoubtedly continue to produce the major number of films.

Distribution

Distributors, the "middlemen" in the filmmaking process, provide the link between the producer and the exhibitor. Along with the distribution companies under the control of the studios, one hundred and ten independent distributors—Vestron, Island, and Cinecom among them—have specialized in distributing independent feature and "art" films and are now investing in production. They are putting money "up-front" with the intention of sharing in the profits. The goal of the distributor in every case is to **position** the film; that is to reach its target audience; the video cassette market has broadened the target audience quite considerably.

In the case of a *theatrical release* film, the distributor begins to publicize it by sending out early press releases on the stars, the location, problems of production, costs. These preliminaries get the film "into the public mind" and create expectations. Once the film is completed, it is **test-marketed**. Everything from preview screenings to telephone surveys of the "product-acceptance" type is used and, depending on the response, an entire advertising campaign, including newspaper coverage and "trailers," is organized. Newspaper coverage involves a range of more detailed news on the production of the film in the daily press and in major magazines. Trailers are advertisements, run on TV and in theatres. The producer-distributors of BROADCAST NEWS (1987), for example, created three different trailers aimed at different audiences, suggesting that the movie was either a comedy, a romance, or a serious behind-the-scenes look at TV news.

The marketing is carefully calculated and is based on a decision about the **release pattern**, defined as *the number and location of the theatres into which a film will be released.* Distributors decide on whether the release will be "fast" or "slow." **Fast release** is, as the name implies, *release of a film to many theatres all at the same time.* It is used by big-budget films designed to be blockbusters (huge and quick box-office successes). "Fast release" costs a great deal because several thousand prints must be made and released, along with massive advertising, to an equal number of theatres. George Lucas's WILLOW and Steven Spielberg's WHO FRAMED ROGER RABBIT? both opened in fast release in the spring of 1988. The object was (and always is in the case of fast release) to take the country by storm, based on the producers' names, their previous successes, and audience expectation).

"Slow release" is used for "smaller" independent features which cannot risk the expenditures on a large number of prints and advertising. Slow release films are usually aimed at a narrower group, a more specific audience and are released first to selected theatres in urban areas. Slow release movies such as JULIA (1977); HESTER STREET (1972); STRANGER THAN PARADISE (1984); DOWN BY LAW (1986); LIVING ON TOKYO TIME (1987); MATEWAN (1987), and a number of other select films, had to rely on word of mouth, good reviews, and eventually Academy Award nominations, but they also required a distributor to place them "correctly."

Exhibition

In the "Golden Age," exhibition meant only *theatrical* release. Cable television and videotape have changed the role of the exhibitor. In addition changing demographics in the United States resulted in the expansion of shopping malls with multiplex theatres. The corporations that own the studios have also invested in theatres and now own over one-fifth of the theatres across the country. What does this do to and for the industry?

The theatres want blockbusters that will keep customers coming for weeks in as many theatres as possible. The exhibitors bid on the films, basing their bids on the studio's advance publicity. "**Blind bidding**," as this practice is called, means that the theatres risk on the studio's production. George Lucas Productions' promise that HOWARD THE DUCK would be as successful as E.T., led to financial troubles when it "bombed." Blind bidding is illegal in many states but exhibitors put up with it because although it is a gamble, the rewards of a blockbuster are huge.

Block booking, the other practice deemed illegal in the '40's, has also benefited from a climate more favorable to corporate power and has "made a comeback." Just as in the past, exhibitors commit themselves to renting the studio's lower budget productions in order to have access to the blockbusters. Filling the theatres with a narrow range of studio productions means that independent features, foreign films, artistic and experimental films, and documentaries are rarely available, especially in smaller communities.

In the 1970's Cable TV briefly threatened exhibitors and led to another wave of theatre closings. Initially it seemed the studios misjudged its potential just as they had underestimated TV twenty years before. But it turns out that after initial interest in Cable, it has not made the same inroads into "audience share" that TV originally made. The staggering impact on exhibition (and therefore on production) has come from the VCR. However, expansion of one area of entertainment tends to help rather than hurt other, related areas. Because of the video cassette player, a new market has been opened for foreign films, the "art" film, and independent features. The increase in demand for films on cassette has increased the number of films produced and exhibited in theatres. Disney, and other studios, own their cable channels and movies are being produced exclusively for those cable networks and others like Home Box Office. They have gone on to produce for the cassette market.

The video cassette market is growing at an amazing rate. More than sixty percent of American households own video cassette recorders and the number continues to increase; video sales and rental stores have cropped up, nearly overnight, in towns all across the country. Video copies are cheaper to produce and easier to circulate than film prints so independent filmmakers, able to find a willing distributor, have the opportunity to reach a public that until now was unavailable to them. Problems of size, shape, and format do interfere with direct transfer from film to TV since television cannot "look" exactly like movies. Films are produced differently when the producer knows that a large portion of profit will eventually come from TV and video sales. The productions are being designed to match TV format and a new transfer process has been developed called "letter-boxing," which keeps the full wide screen image but leaves a dark band at the top and bottom of the video screen. By 1988, THE COLOR PURPLE, INNERSPACE, HANNAH AND HER SISTERS were distributed in "letterbox" format. As video and transfer technology continue to improve and continue to support independent productions, a world of visual material may open up to a public who has never before had access to a range of films.

The Future

Are movie theatres a thing of the past? Certainly the old single-screen theatres and the smaller repertory theatres and art houses in urban areas are either closing, selling to the chains or being turned into multiple-screen theatres. The decade of the eighties was very good for the theatres and the studios, since they are once again permitted to own both the sources of production and the places of exhibition. They are building huge "plexes," multiplexes that is, but in shopping malls throughout rapid population growth areas, especially in the Sun Belt. Although it might be tempting to assume that video and home viewing will be the market of the future (because of the popularity of VCR's and the failure of inner-city theatres), executives are banking on high movie theatre attendance.

The VCR is, however, causing changes in the kind of films being made (as well as changes in the material on TV—the media affect and have impact upon each other). Some of the changes are based on the fact that people watch in the privacy of their homes and this takes entertainment out of the public forum so the material cannot be as easily legislated and controlled by government or media agencies. That, in turn, means a loss of control over ratings and the possibility of a wide variety of material than might otherwise remain unavailable.

Is there a future for an invention like "Dial-a-Film"? Will we see transmission of films over computers or through laser technology? Will there be transmission of films or information via Satellite into homes? Will truly high resolution television screens, which have been promised for many years and are currently being researched in Asia, end the controversy over image quality? A market has already begun to develop for something as simple as home delivery of video cassettes, perhaps soon with pizza.

The fact is that anyone with a VCR can see practically anything anytime. In fact, anyone with a bit of money can own a collection of films on tape. Viewing a film on TV does change the experience—the image is flattened, detail is lost, the image size is not only smaller but in a different proportion, the edges are rounded rather than sharp, scan lines are visible so textures change, color is modified, just to name a few differences—but the success of the VCR testifies to the appeal of individual control over the viewing situation—choice of film, choice of screening time, volume, even food and drink, and, of course, all at more limited expense. For all the negative aesthetic modifications, there are quite a number of attractions. If the choice is between seeing a film on tape or not seeing it at all, what would most people choose? What would you choose?

At the end of EXPLORERS (1985), the kids, who have reached a dwelling in outer space, see that the creatures there have had access to all the film and TV shows of the last several decades as TV has beamed them into space. And what is the result? The extra-terrestrials are film and TV buffs, avid viewers of all the material available on the tube: they speak fluent English (unlike E.T.) but completely based on TV advertisements and programs; they rattle off lines from the ads, "Do you know me? Often when I enter a hotel or restaurant, people fail to recognize me. . . ." and an entire routine for an "amazing kitchen companion that slices, chops, minces," and "makes French fries, shoestrings or crinkle cuts"; they "do" Ed Sullivan, Groucho Marx, Little Richard, W.C. Fields and several other TV comedians.

Hearing all these "canned" lines (with canned laughter) one of the kids, Bennett, worries that "it doesn't make sense." His companion explains "that's the way they think we talk," while behind them TV clips play on a wall-sized screen—Tom and Jerry Cartoons, news programs, the Paramount logo, "I Love Lucy," and other material. An ad for a disinfectant—"Germs!!!! They're all around you . . ."—reminds the space travellers that they had to be disinfected upon arrival. The "girl" alien explains: "we know what you do to our kind down there," and switches the channel to show old sci-fi movies including THE DAY THE EARTH STOOD STILL, GODZILLA, and FLYING SAUCERS FROM MARS, in which the alien creatures are all killed, shot, blown up, attacked by the army. "But that's the movies!" cries Bennett, "that's not the way we really are." The "guy" says to him in his comedian's voice, "you expect me to believe that?" and then gets more serious: "Your people just like to blow things up." Bennett tries to explain that it isn't "real." "We don't really kill people . . . well, we do . . . but not aliens, because . . . we haven't met any." The "guy" makes a plea for understanding, friendship, and tolerance. He says he knows he looks weird to the boys but that they look as weird to him and goes on to say , "I watched four episodes of *Lassie* before I figured out why the little hairy kid never spoke."

When, at the end, the three earthlings are leaving, the "girl" gives Bennett a gem, he asks what it is. The "guy" alien answers in a perfect imitation of Bogart: "It's the stuff dreams are made of." "She" then says in Ingrid Bergman's accents: "We'll always have Paris." Ironically, the kids, themselves already space-travellers need to be "time-travellers", as well; after all, they only recognize the allusions, only "know" the material from the same sources as the "aliens": TV.

So . . . along with rock and roll music, Groucho Marx, W.C. Fields, and old science-fiction films, CASABLANCA and THE MALTESE FALCON have become emblems of our culture and are captured, recorded, and beamed into outer space—or at least into foreign countries where people "think we talk that way" and that we live the way they see it on the TV. What is the message? Movies and TV transmit our culture, our styles, and our values. We might as well be prepared to understand what we are telling others.

Figure 71. CASABLANCA. The film has become a cultural artifact, a symbol in itself of romance and the impossibility of permanence in love.

Afterword: A Critical Eye

I had called on my friend Sherlock Holmes upon the morning after Christmas to wish him the compliments of the season. "I should like, Watson, to go very soon," said Holmes as we sat down to a cup of holiday cheer. "Go! Where to?" "To the Odeon Cinema," said he.

I was not surprised. Indeed my only wonder was that he had not already invited me to accompany him on his excursions to examine this newest art, which was the single topic of interest across the length and breadth of several countries. "I should be most happy to accompany you if I should not be in the way," said I. "My dear Watson. You would confer a great favor upon me by coming. And, from my recent experience, I think that your time will not be mis-spent, for there are points about this new invention which promise to have some bearing on the method I have endeavored to establish. That is, to read from the indications presented, the meaning of the visual evidence."

And so it happened that an hour or so later, I found myself at the Odeon, in the seventh row on the aisle. Holmes, his sharp, eager face outlined in the half light, was seated at my side. As the lights continued to dim even further, the music rose, and I felt rather than saw him settle into his chair, his eyes hooded but alert. . . .

"Do you see, Watson?" Holmes whispered during a momentary lull, "the gambler wearing the black leather gloves is the villain and has committed the murder; the other, wearing the white hat and scarf, is the hero and will discover the culprit." "But Holmes," I protested, "how could you possibly know that?" "Elementary, my dear Watson. Evil and good, you know. To decipher the codes, one must have a critical eye. It is of the utmost importance."

Suggested Readings

Chapter Two

Cheshire, David, *The Book of Movie Photography,* New York, Alfred A. Knopf, 1979.
Finch, Christopher, *Special Effects,* New York, Abbeville Press, 1984.
Lipton, Lenny, *Independent Filmmaking,* San Francisco, Straight Arrow Books, 1972.
Schaefer, Dennis, and Salvato, Larry (eds.), *Masters of Light,* Berkeley, University of Calif. Press, 1984.

Chapter Three

Barr, Tony, *Acting for the Camera,* New York, Harper and Row, 1982.
Barsacq, Leon, *A History of Film Design,* New York, New American Library, Inc. 1978.
McBride, Joseph (ed.), *Filmmakers on Filmmaking* Vol. I and II, Boston, J.P. Tarcher, Inc. 1983.
Ritsko, Alan, *Lighting for Location Motion Pictures,* New York, Van Nostrand Reinhold Co. 1979.

Chapter Four

Burch, Noel, *Theory of Film Practice,* New York, Praeger Pub. 1973.
Eisenstein, Sergei, *Film Form* (Jay Leyda, ed. and trans.), New York, Horcourt, Brace, and World, Inc. 1949.
Pudovkin, V. I, *Film Technique and Film Acting* (Ivor Montague, ed. and trans.), New York, Grove Press, 1960.
Reisz, Karel, *The Technique of Film Editing,* New York, Hastings House, 1968.

Chapter Five

Cameron, Evan W. (ed.), *Sound and the Cinema,* Pleasantville, N.Y., Redgrave, 1980.

Frater, Charles B., *Sound Recording for Motion Pictures*, New York, A.S. Barnes, 1979.

Weis, Elizabeth, and Belton, John (eds.), *Film Sound*, New York, Columbia University Press, 1985.

Yale French Studies, No. 60, 1980. Special issue. (Charles F. Altman, ed.)

Chapter Six

Bordwell, David, Janet Staiger, and Kristi Thompson, *The Classical Hollywood Cinema*, New York, Columbia University Press, 1985.

Eisenstein, Sergei, *Film Form and Film Sense* (Jay Leyda ed. and trans.), New York, Harcourt, Brace and World, Inc. 1949.

Nilsen, Vladimir, *The Cinema as Graphic Art*, New York, Hill and Wang (ISBN paperback edition: 0-8090-1366-5).

Nochlin, Linda, *Realism*, London, Penguin, 1971.

Chapter Seven

Berger, John, *Ways of Seeing*, London, Pelican, 1977.

Dorfman, Ariel, and Armand Mattelart, *How to Read Donald Duck*, London, International General, 1975.

Wollen, Peter, *Signs and Meaning in the Cinema*, Bloomington, Indian University Press, 1972.

Chapter Eight

Balio, Tino (ed.), *The American Film Industry*, University of Wisconsin Press, 1976.

The Hollywood Reporter, Hollywood, California, Issues dating back to 1944.

Litwak, Mark, *Reel Power*, New York, William Morrow & Co. 1986.

Taub, Eric, *Gaffers, Grips, and Best Boys*, New York, St. Martin's Press, 1987.

Glossary

Aerial perspective Also called atmospheric perspective. Closer objects are in greater detail than distant ones which are in soft tones with blurred outlines.
Allusion A mention or indirect reference to something external to the work in which it appears. May be other works of art, books, films or cultural artifacts.
American shot "Plan américain," named by the French. Slightly fuller than a medium shot, it includes the figure from mid-calf.
Angle The position of the camera in relation to the subject.
Angle/reverse angle shot The first shot is followed by another taken from an angle opposite to it.
Art director Also called the set designer. Researches decor and settings; oversees artists, craftspersons, decorators for the creation of a set.
Backlight The light placed behind a subject that separates it from the background.
Blocking Also called choreography. The plotting out of interaction between the movements of the camera and actors.
Blue-screen photography The chemical response of certain film stocks to blue light makes it possible to film a figure against a blue screen and then superimpose the image on another background without the blue screen showing.
Cinematographer Also called the director of photography or D.P. In charge of the camera, s/he selects the lighting, framing, and the set-ups for each shot according to the director's plan.
Close-up The camera records an area in which a person's head (or an object) fills the screen so there is very little background.
Composition The arrangement of visual elements in the shot.
Conforming The cutting and arranging of the original print based on the fine cut of the work print.
Continuity The progression of the narrative, usually based on the logic of the action. Also used to refer to the smooth transition from one shot to the next.
Continuity assistant The person responsible for ensuring visual consistency from shot to shot and sequence to sequence.

Contrast ratio The proportion between darker and lighter parts of a set or location.

Crane shot A shot taken from a camera mounted on a mechanical device that may move freely along a vertical axis. It includes a telescoping arm on which the camera operator sits.

Cross-cut The shots alternate between actions occuring in at least two different locations. It suggests simultaneity and eventual convergence of the actions.

Cultural connotation Understanding based on the things everyone learns about society, ways of living and behaving in a social group, values, assumptions, expectations.

Deep focus Requires a wide angle lens and provides maximum depth of field. It allows the image in the foreground, middleground, and background to remain in focus at the same time.

Depth of field The scope of the image in focus.

Dialogue Lines spoken by characters in conversation.

Director The person in charge of all aspects of the production of a film: acting, set design, cinematography, sound, among other areas.

Dissolve A fade-out superimposed over a fade-in so that one image begins to disappear as the other begins to appear. The dissolve may be quick: over a small number of frames, or slow: over a large number of frames.

Dolly shot The camera films while mounted on a dolly, a miniature crane equipped with wheels.

Dynamic composition The composition of a number of graphic elements in motion It organizes movement within the single shot creating continuous space of cross shots.

Editing Cutting and juxtaposing pieces of film into a specific order to convey meaning.

Establishing shot Shows the whole scene—sets and action in the shot.

Eyeline match The cut is made on the basis of the direction of a character's glance or gaze.

Fade in The camera lens opening is gradually opened so the image brightens from black to normal light. It almost always marks the beginning of a sequence.

Fade out The camera lens opening is gradually closed down so the image darkens to black. It almost always marks the end of a sequence.

Fill light The light used to modify pools of darkness formed between the key lights.

Film noir A French term that refers to the group of gritty, somber thrillers made in the late forties. The lighting is particularly distinctive.

Flash forward A narrative sequence that sets up the action as taking place in the future in relation to the present time of the story.

Flashback A narrative sequence that sets action into the past in relation to the present time of the story.

Flip frame The image seems to turn over to reveal another one.

Focal length The distance between the camera lens and the film. The telephoto shot uses a long focal length; the wide angle shot uses a short focal length.

Focus The degree of sharpness of the image.

Frame One single image on the film strip. Also refers to the edges of the image projected on the screen.

Freeze shot Also called freeze frame. A single frame is reprinted many times so that when projected the shot looks like a still photograph.

Full shot A more confined type of long shot. The figure fills the screen from top to bottom of the frame.

Guillotine splicer A device with a sharp precision cutting blade used to tape-splice film together during editing.

Hairlight A small spotlight placed behind the subject to illuminate the hair and back of the head, producing a halo effect.

High angle shot The camera is placed higher than the subject of the image. It often suggests the subject's helplessness and vulnerability.

Iconography The likeness or image of an actor (or object) which imparts a particular meaning to the shot or film.

Intellectual montage Eisenstein's term for the joining of two images that contain differing, contrasting or seemingly unrelated information to make an abstract idea concrete.

Iris shot A type of masking shot in which an area in the shape of a circle encloses the image.

Jump-cut A slight mismatch between two actions that causes the film to jump slightly from one shot to the next.

Key light The primary source of illumination of a set.

Kuleshov experiment Soviet director Lev Kuleshov's "experiment in editing." By juxtaposing shots of an actor's face with other images, the actor seemed to be responding differently to the material in each shot.

Lens The instrument that controls the size of the subject, the scope of the image, and the range of focus.

Linear perspective Figures meant to be distant are smaller that those meant to be closer.

Location An actual place that serves as the background for the action.

Long shot The camera records an area equal to the height of a standing figure with extensive background, emphasizing the relation between the figure and its surroundings.

Low angle shot The camera is placed lower than the subject of the image and often produces a towering figure or object.

Master shot The entire scene filmed without interruption. Close-ups and other angles are added later.

Match cut The cut is matched on the basis of screen direction, action, graphic elements, or eyeline direction to produce a smooth transition between two shots.

Matte shot Two separate shots are superimposed and printed onto a single piece of film.

Medium shot The camera records an area equal to the height of a seated figure or a figure from the waist up.

Mise en scene A French word referring to the organization and arrangement of everything placed in front of the camera in preparation for filming.

Mix All sounds—dialogue, music, sound effects—on separate tracks are blended electronically into a single track.

Montage The French word for editing. In Hollywood it refers to any sequence of rapidly edited images that suggests the passage of time or events. It sketches but does not develop information about characters. (See *Soviet Montage*.)

Montage of conflict Sergei Eisenstein's style of editing in which images are cut so that they "collide" with one another.

Motif A repeated object, action or phrase associated with a character or situation. The main theme or subject developed and elaborated in a work of art.

Narrative A progression of events related in time and by cause; a story.

Normal lens The lens approximates the scope and size of normal vision. It uses a mid-range focal length.

Oblique angle The camera films from a tilted position.

Pan shot The camera is mounted on a non-moving base and films while pivoting on its axis, along the line of the horizon from left to right or right to left.

Persistence of vision The image stays on the retina of the eye for a split second after the object has disappeared from view.

Point of view Borrowed from literary criticism, the term refers to the "eyes" through which a reader or viewer sees a story or event.

Point of view shot Taken from a distance and angle that represents what a character sees. Also called subjective shot or first person shot.

Process shot Also called rear projection. The pre-photographed background is projected onto a translucent screen and filmed with live action in the foreground.

Rack focussing Also called "pulled focus." The change of focus during a shot without stopping the camera.

Rushes Also called dailies. The footage shot each day of production.

Scene Refers to a sequence in which the action takes place in a single place and time. It also means a specific set of events occurring in a specific location in front of the camera.

Screen direction A character, an object, or the camera moves in a specific direction across the screen. Matching this element establishes continuity.

Sequence A shot or series of shots that present a meaningful unit of action.

Set The "worlds" created in the studio for fiction films.

Set-up Placement of the lights and camera in relation to set, props, and action.

Shooting ratio The amount of film footage finally used in proportion to the amount discarded.

Shot The primary unit of filmmaking. A single uncut length of film.

Slow motion The camera films at a faster rate than the normal 24 frames per second. The image is projected at normal speed so the action looks slow.

Sound effects All sounds that are not dialogue, narration or music. They heighten the illusion of reality. Often ambient or background sound not connected to visible sources.

Sound off Sound whose source is not visible in the images on the screen.

Sound on Sound whose source is visible in the images on the screen; dialogue or noise made by on-screen figures or objects, for example, a record player or a radio.

Sound stage Spaces in which acoustics and lighting of sets and decors may be controlled.

Soviet montage A style of editing distinguished by its use of many shots edited together in sequences of rapidly changing images.

Storyboard A set of sketches that lays out the set-ups of the shots.

Swish pan A pan so rapid that it blurs the image.

Symbol Anything that represents another thing, often a concrete object that stands for an abstract idea.

Take The recording of a shot on film. Each time the shot is filmed it is identified as a "take" by number. For fiction films, shots are often filmed many times.

Telephoto lens A lens that has a long focal length and so has minimum depth of field. It flattens the image.

Textual connotation Meanings that emerge out of the organization of a specific work.

Tracking shot The camera films while it moves parallel to the movement of the subject.

Travelling shot Any shot in which the camera moves while filming.

Voice-over Narration or dialogue spoken off-camera. Often the disembodied voice gives information, offers explanation or description, or tells a story.

Wide angle shot A shot taken with a lens of short focal length that keeps the image in focus from close to the camera to as far as the eye can see.

Wipe One image moves across the screen, pushing off the one already there.

Work print A print of the original filmed footage which is made specifically for editing. After the fine cut or the work print has been completed, the original will be conformed to it.

Zoom shot A shift of focal length during the filming without stopping the camera. It changes the range of focus and the scope of the shot.

Index

Actors and Acting, 4, 15, 17, 34, 37–39, 41, 52, 54–57, 77, 84, 85, 97, 100, 115, 135, 160, 166
Advertisers and Advertising, 1, 4, 8, 9, 11, 54, 63, 68, 89, 124, 127, 137, 139, 169, 170, 173
AIRPLANE, 145
ALIEN, 34
Allen, Woody, 15, 45, 74, 95, 141, 145, 146, 168
Angle, 7, 15, 18–22, 24, 25, 28, 29, 34, 94, 96, 135
Animation, 10, 33, 34, 35, 89, 103
Antonioni, Michelangelo, 48, 111
APOCALYPSE NOW, 53
AUTOMATIC MOVING COMPANY, THE, 33, 34
Avant-garde, 132

Backlighting, 52, 115
BANANAS, 74
BATTERIES NOT INCLUDED, 33
BATTLE OF ALGIERS, THE, 28, 112
BATTLESHIP POTEMKIN, THE, 21, 71, 72, 73, 112, 120
Beatty, Warren, 98
Beaver, Chris, 61
BELIZAIRE THE CAJUN, 169
Bergman, Ingmar, 31, 47, 48, 110, 143
Bertolucci, Bernardo, 47, 144
BIG SLEEP, THE, 50
Blacklist, The, 162, 163, 164
BLACKMAIL, 86
BLADE RUNNER, 42
BLAZING SADDLES, 47, 68
Blindbooking, 160, 170, 171

Block booking, 160, 171
Blocking, 41, 57
BLONDE VENUS, 50
BLUE ANGEL, THE, 54, 56, 86, 87
Blue-screen photography, 35
Bogart, Humphrey, 162, 163, 173
Bogdanovich, Peter, 27
BONNIE AND CLYDE, 28, 44
Boorman, John, 29
BRAZIL, 103
BREATHLESS, 27, 64, 69
BRIGHTON BEACH MEMOIRS, 95
BROADCAST NEWS, 33, 74, 126, 169
BROTHER FROM ANOTHER PLANET, 168
BURDEN OF DREAMS, A, 131

Cable TV, 168, 170, 171
Cahiers du cinema, 50
CASABLANCA, 3, 64, 65, 70, 71, 74, 83, 120, 140, 174
CATCH-22, 31, 34
Chandler, Raymond, 80
Chaplin, Charlie, 18, 32, 55
CHILDREN OF PARADISE, THE, 128
CHINA SYNDROME, THE, 56
CHINATOWN, 49, 55
CHOOSE ME, 69
Cinecom, 169
CinemaScope, 164
Cinematographer, 14, 15, 18, 25, 37, 38, 47, 49, 51, 52, 53
Cinerama, 164
CITIZEN KANE, 19, 22, 23, 49, 53, 71, 87, 98, 99, 128, 143

Close-up, 15, 16, 18, 22, 25, 29, 31, 57, 59, 64, 65, 70, 72, 77, 115, 120, 121, 143, 145, 147, 158
Cohl, Emil, 34
Coppola, Francis, 37, 47, 168
Crane shot, 25, 27, 94
CRIES AND WHISPERS, 31, 48
Cross-cutting, 123

DARK CIRCLE, 17, 29, 61, 72, 131
Davis, Peter, 123
DAY THE EARTH STOOD STILL, THE, 173
DEFENSE OF THE REALM, 71
DeNiro, Robert, 20
DePalma, Brian, 74, 145
Deren, Maya, 132, 133, 134
DESPERATELY SEEKING SUSAN, 104
DIAL M FOR MURDER, 164
Dietrich, Marlene, 49, 50
Distribution, 159, 160, 165, 166, 168, 169
Documentary, 10, 16, 17, 28, 30, 38, 42, 54, 89, 96, 98, 100, 102, 123, 124, 125, 128, 131, 133, 134, 171
DOLCE VITA, LA, 92
DOUBLE INDEMNITY, 49, 50, 99
Dynamation, 35

ECLIPSE, 111
Eisenstein, Sergei, 47, 71, 74, 135, 136, 145
EL NORTE, 169
Establishing shot, 62, 65, 66, 67, 82
Exhibitors, 84, 160, 170, 171
EXPLORERS, 173

Falk, Peter, 99
FANNY AND ALEXANDER, 48
FATAL ATTRACTION, 33
Fellini, Federico, 92
Ferrero, Pat, 38, 100, 131, 134
Film Noir, 45, 50, 51, 92

FITZCARRALDO, 131
Flaherty, Robert, 134
Flashback, 6, 31, 68, 70, 71, 74, 80, 89, 140
FLYING SAUCERS FROM MARS, 173
Focal length, 28
Fonda, Jane, 56, 145
Ford, John, 20, 91, 92, 142, 153
Foreground, 29, 34, 70, 107, 115, 155
400 BLOWS, THE, 27, 32
Framing, 76, 80
Frankenheimer, John, 20, 22
Freeze frame, 32

GANDHI, 26
Garbo, Greta, 55
Genre, 42, 46, 53, 61, 126, 127, 128, 132, 134, 161
German Expressionism, 49
Godard Jean-Luc, 27, 64, 69, 145
GODFATHER, THE, 44, 49
GODZILLA, 173
GOLD RUSH, THE, 18, 31, 32
Gorbman, Claudia, 90
GRADUATE, THE, 29
GRAND ILLUSION, THE, 128
Griffith, D. W., 15, 59, 67

Hagman, Larry, 54
Hand-held camera, 27
HANNAH AND HER SISTERS, 171
HAROLD AND MAUDE, 3
Harryhausen, Ray, 35
Harvey, Lawrence, 20, 27
HEARTS AND HANDS, 100, 131
HEARTS AND MINDS, 123
Hellinger, Mark, 102
Herrmann, Bernard, 92, 93
HESTER STREET, 170
Heston, Charlton, 88, 121
HISTORY LESSONS, 46

Hitchcock, Alfred, 20, 21, 25, 27, 31, 34, 37, 41, 42, 45, 57, 61, 64, 67, 77, 86, 92, 103, 164
Hoffmann, Dustin, 29, 99, 147
HOLLYWOOD SHUFFLE, 168
Holmes, Karen, 13, 35, 133, 134
HOPE AND GLORY, 29
HOWARD THE DUCK, 170
HUAC, 162, 164

Ince, Thomas, 15
INNERSPACE, 171
INTERMEZZO, 74
Iris shot, 68
Irving, Judy, 38, 61, 131
ISHTAR, 128
IVAN THE TERRIBLE, 47

Jarmusch, Jim, 38, 168
JAZZ SINGER, THE, 88
JEAN DE FLORETTE, 128
JEREMIAH JOHNSON, 63
JETEE, LA, 71
Jolson, Al, 88
JULIA, 56, 170
Jump-Cut, 69

KOUMIKO MYSTERY, THE, 100
Kuleshov, Lev, 77, 78, 90

LADY IN THE LAKE, THE, 80
LAST EMPEROR, THE, 47, 53
LAST LAUGH, THE, 24, 29, 47, 53, 56
LAWRENCE OF ARABIA, 127
Lee, Spike, 168
LIANNA, 168
LIFE AND TIMES OF ROSIE THE RIVETER, THE, 67
Lighting, 115, 124, 132, 135, 138, 144
LITTLE BIG MAN, 92, 99, 135, 146–158
LIVING DAYLIGHTS, THE, 97, 102
LONEDALE OPERATOR, THE, 67

Lorre, Peter, 91
Lucas, George, 37, 95, 168, 170
Lumiere, Louis, 25
LUNA, 47

MAGNIFICENT AMBERSONS, THE, 30, 41
MALTESE FALCON, THE, 174
MANCHURIAN CANDIDATE, THE, 20, 22, 24, 31, 32, 68, 145
MANON OF THE SPRINGS, 128
Marker, Chris, 100, 102
MATEWAN, 52, 168, 170
Matte, 34, 35
MCCABE AND MRS. MILLER, 97, 98
McCarthyism, 162
Melies, Georges, 34
Melodrama, 127
MESHES OF THE AFTERNOON, 132
Middleground, 29, 107, 111, 115
MISHIMA, 42, 49
MISSING, 145, 152
Montage, 74, 123
MOONSTRUCK, 33
Motif, 21, 91, 92, 94, 133, 144, 145, 150, 151, 156, 157
MTV, 2, 89, 104
Murnau, F. W., 24

NAKED CITY, THE, 102
Narration, 11, 88, 89, 98, 99, 100, 102, 131, 147
Narrative, 6, 10, 21, 24, 31, 93, 98, 99, 104, 105, 118, 124, 125, 126, 128, 131, 132, 133, 134, 135, 136, 141, 142, 144, 147, 152, 158
Narrator, 80, 81, 83, 98, 99, 100, 102
Newman, Paul, 56
Nichols, Mike, 31
Nicholson, Jack, 55
NIGHT MUST FALL, 17

NINE TO FIVE, 145
NOTORIOUS, 24, 25, 34, 67, 77

OCTOBER, 123
Odessa Steps Sequence, The, 71, 72, 74

Panning, 63, 70
Paramount, 165
PEGGY SUE GOT MARRIED, 71
Penn, Arthur, 28, 135, 146–158
PENNIES FROM HEAVEN, 146
PERILS OF PAULINE, THE, 67
Perspective, 7
PINK FLOYD: THE WALL, 104
Pixillation, 33
Pontecorvo, Gillo, 28, 112
POSTMAN ALWAYS RINGS TWICE, THE, 50, 99
PRINCESS BRIDE, THE, 97, 99
PRIZZI'S HONOR, 56
Producers and Producing, 33, 34, 71, 85, 103, 107, 111, 151, 166, 168, 169
PSYCHO, 20, 21, 22, 64, 68, 93, 94, 95
PURPLE ROSE OF CAIRO, THE, 171
Puttnam, David, 71

RAIDERS OF THE LOST ARK, 128, 165
RAMBO, 145
Realism, 6, 53, 71, 98, 103, 104, 111
Rear projection, 34
REAR WINDOW, 77
Redford, Robert, 56, 63, 169
Reiner, Rob, 7
REPO MAN, 104
RETURN OF THE SECAUCUS 7, THE, 168
ROCKY HORROR PICTURE SHOW, 4, 10
ROMANCING THE STONE, 128

ROPE, 41
Rota, Nino, 92
Rotoscope, 35
Rozsa, Miklos, 92
RULES OF THE GAME, THE, 49

SANS SOLEIL, 100
SATURDAY NIGHT FEVER, 145
SAVING THE PROOF, 13, 35, 133, 134
Sayles, John, 38, 52, 168
SCARFACE, 44
SCHOOL DAZE, 168
Schrader, Paul, 42
Schufftan, Eugen, 34
Scorcese, Martin, 27
SEARCHERS, THE, 44
SERPENT'S EGG, THE, 103
SEVENTH SEAL, THE, 48, 49
SEVENTH VOYAGE OF SINBAD, THE, 35
SHANGHAI EXPRESS, 50
Sharman, Jim, 4
SHE'S GOTTA HAVE IT, 99, 168
Shot-reverse shot, 96, 124
SILKWOOD, 44
SILVERADO, 44, 127
SINGIN' IN THE RAIN, 85, 86
SOLDIER BLUE, 151, 157
Sound-track, 91, 94, 95
Soviet montage, 71, 77
SPACEBALLS, 146
SPARTACUS, 163
Spielberg, Steven, 168
STAGECOACH, 91, 92, 127
STAND BY ME, 6, 7, 10, 71
Stars, 2, 54, 55, 56, 71
STAR WARS, 33, 34, 36, 46, 49, 54, 55, 57, 83
Stewart, James, 43, 77, 78
Storaro, Vincent, 47, 53
STRADA, LA, 92
Straub, Jean-Marie, 46

SUNSET BOULEVARD, 99
Swish pan, 24

TAMPOPO, 69
Telephoto, 28, 29
Television, 1–11, 19, 20, 32, 39, 55, 63, 68, 71, 89, 120, 121, 124, 125, 159, 161, 164, 165, 170–172
3:10 to YUMA, THE, 141, 142, 144
Todd-AO, 120
TOUCH OF EVIL, 88, 121
Townsend, Robert, 168
Tracking, 25, 27
Transitions, 31
TREASURE OF THE SIERRA MADRE, THE, 128
Trinh T. Minh-ha, 38, 66, 102, 133, 134
TRIP TO BOUNTIFUL, THE, 169
TRON, 34
Truffaut, Francois, 27, 32

UNTOUCHABLES, THE, 20, 44, 74

VCR, 94, 171, 172
VERTIGO, 31, 34, 42, 77
Video, 1, 3, 11, 63, 90, 104, 105, 121, 159, 166, 169, 171, 172
VIRGIN SPRING, THE, 48
VistaVision, 164
Voice-over, 6, 98, 99, 100, 102, 131
Von Sternberg, Joseph, 42, 49, 54, 86

Wayne, John, 20, 55, 91, 162
WELFARE, 131
Welles, Orson, 22, 41, 50, 87, 92, 100, 103, 121
Westerns, 10, 61, 63, 91, 92, 105, 106, 127, 161
Wexler, Haskell, 52
WILLOW, 170
WINCHESTER '73, 141, 145
Wiseman, Frederick, 131
WITCHES OF EASTWICK, THE, 34

YOUNG MR. LINCOLN, 20, 27, 32